S0-AAH-669

All Around the Town

This is where George Washington took the oath of office as the first President of the United States in 1789—the U.S. Treasury building on Wall Street, downtown New York.

All Around the Town

A NEW YORK COOKBOOK

*With Hundreds of
Recipes from New York's
Finest Restaurants*

by **CEIL DYER**
and **ROSALIND COLE**

THE BOBBS-MERRILL COMPANY, INC.
Indianapolis   New York

The Bobbs-Merrill Company, Inc.
Indianapolis · New York
Copyright © 1972 by Ceil Dyer and Rosalind Cole
All rights reserved
Library of Congress Catalogue Card Number: 77-173214
Designed by Jack Jaget
Manufactured in the United States of America

Contents

PART III—*German and Middle European Food*

PART IV—*Russian Food*

PART V—*Greek and Near and Middle Eastern Food*

PART VI—*Asian Food*

PART VII—*Mexican and Latin-American Food*

PART VIII—*American Food*

CONTENTS   9

Introduction

NEW YORK is a tourist paradise, no matter whether you are a visitor or you live here year round. The museums are marvelous; theatres, despite their high cost, are exciting; shopping is the best and most varied in the world; and the restaurants—ah, the restaurants. Well, if you are the kind of tourist I am, you'll never stop touring New York's restaurants.

No other city in the world quite prepares one for the overwhelming fact of New York—overwhelming in size and overwhelming in its complexity. Perhaps it is because no other city is such a rich mix of nationalities—so many tongues; so many traditions, each stamped with individuality, yet each a section of the variegated tapestry we call New York.

In a tapestry the whole is a sum of many parts, each color of thread distinct on its own yet each a blend of the whole. So it is here, where the threads of many nations weave an intricate pattern. Where else would St. Patrick's Day and the Fourth of July be celebrated with equal fervor? Where else would there be a mass turnout for the German Steuben Day, for Puerto Rican Day, for Hibernian Day? Where else would the French tricolor appear as if by magic from thousands of windows when the *France* sailed out of New York Harbor for the first time? Where

Manhattan Island as seen from the Pan-Am Building looking south, with the Hudson on the right, the East River on the left, and Staten Island in

the distance. The Empire State Building's spire is in the foreground.

else indeed could it happen? But happen it does in this city, for, though New York has absorbed many cultures and many races, those cultures and races have not been absorbed by New York.

It is this wonderful independence, this acceptance of the right to be different, that New Yorkers cherish. If your mode of life, your clothes, your speech and even your cuisine are different from your neighbor's, you are not looked upon with disfavor; in fact, your neighbor hardly looks at all. It's your business—and rightly so. It is this marvelous tolerance, this acceptance of your right to be different that gives New York its special flavor, its endless variety, its intricate pattern, its never-ending fascination.

It has been said that you can buy anything in New York. Well, when it comes to food, the saying is true. There are Latin markets where akee and plantains are as common as potatoes and peas; *tortillas,* tamales, beans and chilies are easily at hand; and if one is in need of soybean curd, wooden ear, ginger root, rice wine or a sauce made from plums, a telephone call will bring it to your door. Nor is it difficult to locate the specialties of France, Germany, England, India or Norway—they are here because the people are here, the heady mix of many nationalities that is the magic of New York.

To dine well in Paris is easy, but only if you want fine French food. But to eat the best in New York is to select a cuisine—any cuisine—then go to the restaurant of your choice. Greek, Italian, Chinese, Lebanese, Japanese or French, they're all here, and there are others, many others. What's more, in almost all of these so-called foreign establishments the food will be not only good and sometimes great, but also authentic.

And what better way to learn how to cook than to see and taste a dish first as it should be prepared and served? There isn't any, and that's how this book began.

This is not an attempt at a guidebook or to cover each and every eating establishment in New York; rather, it is a personal collection of favorite places and food. There are undoubtedly at least twice as many good restaurants and cafés as we have listed here, but these are the ones we tried and liked, went back and tried again—our little black book, if you will, of where we have dined well in an ambience of good food and good friendship.

Everybody knows Yonah Shimmel's on Houston Street, on the Lower East Side, where you can still get the best potato and kasha knishes in New York.

What we *have* tried to do is cover the varied nationalities that make up New York, and would you believe it, we only ran into trouble when we searched out real American food! The American restaurants, we discovered, were run by people of diverse backgrounds—Irish, Italian, English, French—or the owner was of Italian descent, the chef was from Puerto Rico and the captain was French. Generally speaking, we singled out as "American" those restaurants which were this type of happy blend, where the cuisine was its own interpretation of classic recipes and variations on the same, where the best of numerous cuisines became one—and then we realized that that really is what American cooking is all about.

Happy, adventurous eating! We hope our book will add to your pleasure at home and abroad in this most fascinating of cities—New York.

Restaurants

À La Fourchette
Arirang Korean Restaurant
Asia de Cuba
The Athenian Restaurant
Baroque
Beirut Restaurant
Benihana of Tokyo
Brazilian Coffee Restaurant
Brittany du Soir
Budapest Hungarian Restaurant
Café Brittany
Café de France
Café Manila
Café Verdi
The Camel's Hump
Casa Brasil Restaurant

Cedars of Lebanon

Chalet Suisse

Charley O's Bar & Grill & Bar

Cheshire Cheese Restaurant

Chez Napoleon

Clos Normand

The Coach House

Cookery Lafayette, Inc.

Copenhagen

Dardanelles Armenian Restaurant

Dionysos Restaurant

El Parador Café

Eva Hungarian Restaurant

Fornos

The Forum of the Twelve Caesars

Frini Flamenco Restaurant

Grotta Azzurra Inn

Hellenic Palace

Ho Ho Restaurant

India House East Restaurant

Jai Alai

The Jamaican Restaurant

John Barleycorn

Karachi Restaurant

Kegon Japanese Restaurant

La Cabana

La Famille Restaurant

La Petite Ferme

La Taza de Oro

Lam Kee Restaurant

Le Chambertin

Le Pavillon

Lotus Eaters Royale
Luchow's
The Mandarin House
Marchi's
New Austrian Village Restaurant
New Korea
Oscar's Delmonico Restaurant
Pagoda
Pancho Villa's Mexican Restaurant
Paolucci's
The Philippine Garden
Pierre au Tunnel
Praha Restaurant
Rajmahal Restaurant
René Pujol Restaurant
Russian Bear
Russian Tea Room
Saito Restaurant
San Marco
Scandia
Sign of the Dove
Sloppy Louie's Restaurant
Souvlaki
The Spanish Pavilion
Stockholm Restaurant
Stouffer's
Sweet's Restaurant
Swiss Center Restaurant
Szechuan Village
Trattoria
21 Club
Vasata

Restaurants by Ethnic Group

AMERICAN

The Coach House
Cookery Lafayette, Inc.
La Famille Restaurant
The Forum of the Twelve Caesars
Oscar's Delmonico Restaurant
Sign of the Dove
Sloppy Louie's Restaurant
Stouffer's
Sweet's Restaurant
21 Club

CHINESE

Ho Ho Restaurant
Lam Kee Restaurant
Lotus Eaters Royale
The Mandarin House

Pagoda
Szechuan Village

ENGLISH AND IRISH

Charley O's Bar & Grill & Bar
Cheshire Cheese Restaurant
John Barleycorn

FILIPINO

Café Manila
The Philippine Garden

FRENCH

À La Fourchette
Baroque
Brittany du Soir
Café Brittany
Café de France
Chez Napoleon
Clos Normand
La Petite Ferme
Le Chambertin
Le Pavillon
Pierre au Tunnel
René Pujol Restaurant

GERMAN AND MIDDLE EUROPEAN

Budapest Hungarian Restaurant
Eva Hungarian Restaurant
Luchow's
New Austrian Village Restaurant
Praha Restaurant
Vasata

GREEK
The Athenian Restaurant
Dionysos Restaurant
Hellenic Palace

INDIAN AND PAKISTANI
India House East Restaurant
Karachi Restaurant
Rajmahal Restaurant

ITALIAN
Café Verdi
Grotta Azzurra Inn
Marchi's
Paolucci's
San Marco
Trattoria

JAPANESE
Benihana of Tokyo
Kegon Japanese Restaurant
Saito Restaurant

KOREAN
Arirang Korean Restaurant
New Korea

LATIN-AMERICAN
Asia de Cuba
Brazilian Coffee Restaurant
Casa Brasil Restaurant
Frini Flamenco Restaurant
The Jamaican Restaurant

La Cabana
La Taza de Oro

MEXICAN

El Parador Café
Pancho Villa's Mexican Restaurant

NEAR AND MIDDLE EASTERN

Beirut Restaurant
The Camel's Hump
Cedars of Lebanon
Dardanelles Armenian Restaurant
Souvlaki

RUSSIAN

Russian Bear
Russian Tea Room

SCANDINAVIAN

Copenhagen
Scandia
Stockholm Restaurant

SPANISH

Fornos
Jai Alai
The Spanish Pavilion

SWISS

Chalet Suisse
Swiss Center Restaurant

Restaurants by Location

FINANCIAL DISTRICT

Oscar's Delmonico
Sloppy Louie's Restaurant
Souvlaki
Sweet's Restaurant

CHINATOWN

Lam Kee Restaurant
Pagoda

GREENWICH VILLAGE

Café Verdi
The Camel's Hump
The Coach House
Cookery Lafayette, Inc.
Dardanelles Armenian Restaurant
Jai Alai

The Jamaican Restaurant
La Petite Ferme
The Mandarin House
Souvlaki
Szechuan Village

LOWER EAST SIDE (*Below 14th Street*)

Grotta Azzurra Inn
Paolucci's
Rajmahal Restaurant
Souvlaki

DOWNTOWN EAST SIDE
(*14th Street to 34th Street*)

Cedars of Lebanon
Luchow's
Marchi's
The Philippine Garden
Souvlaki

DOWNTOWN WEST SIDE
(*14th Street to 34th Street*)

Asia de Cuba
Beirut Restaurant
Hellenic Palace
La Taza de Oro

MIDTOWN EAST SIDE
(*34th Street to 72nd Street*)

Baroque
Benihana of Tokyo
Café Manila

Chalet Suisse

Clos Normand

Dionysos Restaurant

El Parador Café

India House East Restaurant

John Barleycorn

Kegon Japanese Restaurant

La Cabana

Le Pavillon

Lotus Eaters Royale

New Korea

Russian Bear

Sign of the Dove

Stouffer's

The Spanish Pavilion

Trattoria

MIDTOWN WEST SIDE
(*34th Street to 72nd Street*)

À La Fourchette

Arirang Korean Restaurant

The Athenian Restaurant

Benihana of Tokyo

Brazilian Coffee Restaurant

Brittany du Soir

Café Brittany

Café de France

Charley O's Bar & Grill & Bar

Cheshire Cheese Restaurant

Chez Napoleon

Copenhagen

Fornos

The Forum of the Twelve Caesars
Ho Ho Restaurant
Karachi Restaurant
Le Chambertin
Pierre au Tunnel
René Pujol Restaurant
Russian Tea Room
Saito Restaurant
San Marco
Scandia
Stockholm Restaurant
Swiss Center Restaurant
21 Club

UPTOWN EAST SIDE

Budapest Hungarian Restaurant
Casa Brasil Restaurant
Eva Hungarian Restaurant
New Austrian Village Restaurant
Pancho Villa's Mexican Restaurant
Praha Restaurant
Vasata

UPTOWN WEST SIDE

Frini Flamenco Restaurant

HARLEM

La Famille Restaurant

All Around the Town

A pretty place to dine, the flower-filled Sign of the Dove, on New York's upper Third Avenue, the scene of some of Jackie Kennedy's famous parties.

PART I

Continental Food

Chapter I

FRENCH FOOD

~~~~~~

Restaurants and Recipes

EVER SINCE New York's first restaurant opened, in 1830, a menu replete with French dishes has been considered by some to be the height of cuisine.

But despite the love of French menus with their *foie* and *fraises, meunière* and *marinière,* the food served in this city's outstanding restaurants before 1940 could better be described as Continental rather than truly French. It was not until the arrival of Henri Soulé from France in 1939 that true *haute cuisine française* really took root—and deeply—in New York. From these seeds, sown by M. Soulé at his Pavillon, other French restaurants began to sprout throughout the city.

Today, with about 40,000 Frenchmen scattered throughout New York, French food can be had in many areas. But the majority of good French restaurants are clustered in midtown Manhattan. On the fashionable East Side are the elegant and expensive restaurants dedicated to the epicurean delights of Gallic high cuisine.

But for the true essence of the French bistro and small inn as they are in France, go to the West Side, to the Forties and Fifties

Sidewalk artist at work in the West Village during the annual

Greenwich Village art show.

between Seventh and Ninth Avenues. There, in small, unpretentious, intimate settings where the chefs, barmen, waiters and waitresses keep up a mellifluous chatter in French, the food is always good and often exceptional, the prices are sensible and the ambience is the next best thing to a trip to France.

CUISINE FRANÇAISE

Although the French is perhaps the most civilized food in the world, the art of fine French cooking is relatively new compared to that of the Orient or even the Near East. It was not until Catherine de Medici arrived in France from Florence with her Italian chefs that French cuisine rose from the level of dining on whatever the day's hunt had produced.

But never had seed fallen on more fertile land. France, more than any other country, produces the finest ingredients that a talented chef could desire. A benign climate, a variety of good soils and ample rainfall, coupled with people who to this day regard farming as a noble profession, result in superb meats and chickens, the best eggs, fabulous cheeses, cream and milk and the freshest, most beautiful produce in the world. When you add an abundance of excellent wine, who wouldn't become interested in raising cooking to an art?

Nonetheless French cooking is essentially simple and has its roots in the thrifty French character. The most apparently complicated sauce is in reality based on good stock, the stock pot that turns American "throwaways" into Sauce Español or Béchamel. Scraps of meat, bones and vegetables that would usually be thrown out are simmered for hours, strained and refrigerated, then used to add flavor to the simplest foods.

Because France is small and still largely agricultural, superbly fresh food is taken for granted. Few Frenchwomen shop for several meals at a time. The French housewife (or her maid) shops for today's foods today. *Les haricots verts* for dinner tonight were growing in the field yesterday. This regard for fresh ingredients is one of the secrets of French cuisine. The just-killed chicken, the fish that was swimming this morning, the egg and cream that have never felt the cold breath of the refrigerator are more important than the most complicated recipe.

The French eat far more lightly than most people think. *Café au lait* and croissants are the average breakfast; lunch is, more often than not, *hors d'oeuvre varié* (a mixture of cold marinated vegetables), a small piece of roast chicken or an entrecote (small broiled steak), cheese and fruit for dessert. Dinner usually includes a soup, fish of some sort, a meat or chicken course, salad and cheese. Portions are small by American standards. One rather small chicken serves a family of six.

Cooking methods vary, but they are based on fine French logic. If the meat is not so tender, then it is made into Boeuf Bourguignon, the red wine acting as a tenderizer through the long, slow cooking. If it is a delicate entrecote, it is quickly broiled and spread with sweet butter creamed with parsley. The classic bouillabaisse of Marseilles evolved from an abundance of assorted fish left over from the morning's sales.

Delicate fish is poached in white wine and covered with a fresh cream sauce because that's what brings out its flavor best. Moules Marinières are simply fresh mussels steamed in white wine, the sauce thickened with a little flour and butter. Vegetables are quickly blanched to preserve their fresh taste, then drenched in sweet butter—what else? Essentially French cooking is a combination of regard for fresh ingredients and a talent for making the best of what's on hand.

Most important, the Frenchman cares about food. It is serious business, but it is not big business as it is here in the States. There are no "Mammoth Food, Inc." but hundreds of devoted bakers, poultrymen, butchers, farmers and dairymen who literally put their soul into their work. If you don't believe this, visit Paris and wander into Fouchon's, that paradisiacal market near the Madeleine to see the intent, almost fanatical devotion paid to every foodstuff from a humble wire rack of eggs to a display of queenly *pâté de foie gras.* Or visit the bakery of Pierre Poilane to have the flour-dusted M. Poilane tell you personally why he makes the best bread in the world, then come home with the sure knowledge that there are no secret ingredients or tricks of the trade in fine French food but love and devotion to good cooking and *la bonne vie.*

One of the few lady cabbies of the horse-drawn carriage set, which makes its stand on 59th Street and Fifth Avenue near the fashionable and venerable Plaza Hotel.

LE PAVILLON

111 East 57th Street   *PL 3-8388*

Le Pavillon—a restaurant in the grand tradition. Here is the very heart and soul of France. No attempt at flashy "catch the eye" decoration, God forbid. Simply the luxe pale boiseried walls, glittering chandeliers, snowy table linen and, of course, flowers, fresh flowers everywhere. The real star is the food, the true *haute cuisine* of France in all its glory, and it is glorious indeed.

Le Pavillon was the creation of the late Henri Soulé, a formidable man who could wither a busboy or a bourgeois would-be diner with a passing glance but who loved Le Pavillon, and he lavished on it the care, time and devotion that are the secret ingredients of a great restaurant. Contrary to some rather unkind rumors, one did not have to be either rich or famous to be welcomed; one did have to have respect for Le Pavillon; M. Soulé simply would not tolerate a casual attitude. Reservations, correct dress and, above all, respect for the cuisine were what he demanded; there were no exceptions.

When Soulé died in early 1967, there were dour predictions that Le Pavillon would die too, but happily it has found a new lover, Stuart Levin, the present owner, who has the same devotion to the cause, the same intent regard for every detail, the same love for *la cuisine*. One can still enjoy one of the greatest of civilized pleasures, the *haute cuisine* of France in a setting that is worthy of the art.

Reservations and a generous wallet are still very much necessities.

Le Pavillon is open for lunch and dinner five days a week. Dinner only on Saturday. Closed on Sunday, and on Saturday during the summer months.

OEUFS A LA NEIGE

4   cups milk
1   vanilla bean or 1 teaspoon vanilla extract

½   cup sugar
6   eggs, separated
¾   cup sugar
     Caramel: ½ cup sugar, ¼ cup water

Pour milk into 9-inch skillet. Add vanilla and the ½ cup of sugar. Place over low heat until bubbles begin to appear around edges of the milk, stirring until sugar is dissolved. Beat egg whites until stiff but not dry. Gradually beat in ¾ cup of sugar until meringue is shiny and very stiff. Shape into ovals. Drop a few at a time into barely simmering milk. Cook about a minute on each side, turning gently with a slotted spoon, until firm to the touch. Drain on paper towels and let cool. Strain milk in which meringues were cooked; remove vanilla bean. Beat egg yolks until light and lemon-colored. Gradually add milk, stirring constantly. Cook over low heat, stirring until custard thickens and coats spoon. Cool custard; strain and chill. Pour custard into crystal bowl and float meringues on top.

In small heavy skillet melt ½ cup sugar, stirring constantly with wooden spoon. Remove from heat and slowly add the water. Return to low heat and simmer until syrup is slightly thick and smooth. Trickle over meringues. Chill thoroughly.

Makes 8 servings.

CLOS NORMAND

42 East 52nd Street   *PL 3-3348*

One of the freshest, prettiest restaurants in town with its Norman half-timbered walls and copper bowls of fresh flowers everywhere. Clos Normand is also one of the best French Provincial restaurants in New York.

Norman specialties head the menu, but the chef includes other provinces as well in his repertoire, and they are excellent indeed.

Luncheon is served from noon to 3 P.M.; dinner from 5:30 to 10:30. Dinner only on Saturday. Closed Sunday.

QUICHE DU CLOS

Pastry for 9-inch pie plate
1 egg white, beaten
¼ cup cooked crab meat
¼ cup cooked lobster meat, cut into small pieces
⅛ teaspoon saffron
1 teaspoon chopped pimento
5 eggs
1½ cups milk
⅛ teaspoon cayenne pepper
½ teaspoon paprika

Preheat oven to 450° F.

Line 9-inch pie plate with pastry and brush with beaten egg white.

Combine crab meat, lobster, saffron and pimentos. Spread over bottom of pie plate. Beat eggs lightly, combine with milk, blend in cayenne pepper and paprika and pour over crab meat–lobster mixture.

Bake at 450° F. for 10 minutes, then lower heat to 350° and bake for 20 to 25 minutes longer or until custard has set and a knife inserted near the center comes out clean. Serve warm.

Serves 6.

FILET DE SOLE DU CHEF

4 to 6 shallots, finely minced
1 tablespoon butter
1½ cups Chablis
8 filets of sole
1 tablespoon butter
2 teaspoons flour
½ cup heavy cream
½ cup fresh orange sections
½ cup fresh pineapple cut into small chunks
Juice of half a lemon
1 banana sliced in rounds

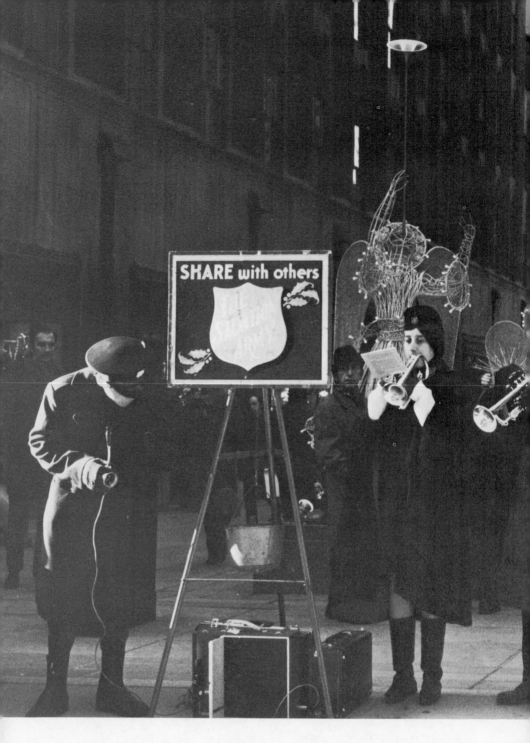

The Salvation Army spreading the word during the festive Yuletide season at Rockefeller Center. The world-famous decorated tree can

be seen in the background.

Preheat oven to 350° F. Sauté the shallots in one tablespoon of butter. Place the filets in a deep, heavy sauté pan. Cover with Chablis and poach over medium heat until fish is done and flakes easily with a fork. Transfer filets to a hot ovenproof platter. Reduce the wine to half by cooking over medium heat for 5 to 10 minutes. Cream together the butter and flour, add to wine stock and mix well. Add the cream and blend well. Cook over low heat until sauce thickens; do not allow to boil. Pour over filets and place in oven for 5 to 10 minutes or until lightly browned. Garnish with orange and pineapple pieces and the rounds of bananas which have first been dipped into the lemon juice to prevent darkening. Serve at once.

Serves 4–6.

NOISETTES DE VEAU NORMAND

8	scallops of veal about ½ inch thick (cut from rib chops)
3	tablespoons butter
¼	cup Calvados
⅛	teaspoon salt
⅛	teaspoon white pepper
½	cup heavy cream
¼	pound fresh mushrooms, sliced
1	tablespoon butter

Sauté the scallops of veal over medium-high heat in the 3 tablespoons of butter until delicately browned. Warm the Calvados in a pan of hot water. Pour excess fat from scallops and flame meat with warm Calvados. This is easily done if the Calvados is poured over the meat while it is still very hot and immediately lighted with a match. When the flame subsides, shake and scrape the pan to loosen brown particles. Add salt, pepper and cream, and continue cooking over low heat for 10 to 15 minutes longer. Do not allow to boil. While meat is cooking, sauté mushrooms in the remaining butter and add to the meat and cream sauce just before serving.

Serves 4.

LE CHAMBERTIN

348 West 46th Street   *PL 7-2154*

With one of the most impressive cellars in New York—over
10,000 bottles dating back to 1949—owner Louis Daniel can
proudly suggest the perfect wine for each dish of his classic
French cuisine.

Charming, quiet and reasonable, Le Chambertin is probably
one of the best restaurant "buys" in the city.

Le Chambertin serves lunch from noon to 2:30 P.M. and dinner from 5:00 P.M. to 9:30 P.M. Closed Sunday.

LE BOEUF BRAISE CHAMBERTIN

6	pounds short ribs of beef, trimmed of most fat and cut into serving pieces
	Salt
	Pepper
	Flour
¼	pound salt pork, diced
3	carrots, scraped and finely chopped
¼	small green pepper, seeded and finely chopped
3	small white onions, peeled and chopped
3	ribs celery, finely chopped
3	cloves garlic, peeled and minced
3	shallots, peeled and minced
2	tablespoons Cognac or other fine brandy
3	cups Burgundy wine
	Beef stock as needed
3	sprigs parsley
1	bay leaf
3	sprigs fresh thyme
2	tablespoons Worcestershire sauce
12	fresh mushrooms
2	tablespoons butter
12	small white onions, peeled

Sprinkle beef with salt and pepper; dredge lightly with flour.
Arrange in a long, shallow well-greased baking pan and place in

a preheated 500° F. oven until well browned. Turn each piece of meat while roasting so that it is well browned on all sides. Remove meat from oven and set aside.

Place diced pork in a large ovenproof saucepan and cook over moderate heat until crisp and well browned. Remove with slotted spoon to paper toweling to drain; set aside.

Sauté in the remaining fat, until soft and golden in color, the carrots, green pepper, onion, celery, garlic, shallots. Add the browned beef and stir to blend; then pour in the Cognac and touch with a lighted match to ignite. Remove from heat and let flame go out.

In a separate saucepan bring wine to a full boil; pour over beef. Add enough beef stock to cover meat.

Tie together the parsley, bay leaf, thyme; add to meat. Cover saucepan and place in a preheated 350° F. oven for 2 hours or until beef is tender.

Remove meat and place in a glass or other nonmetal storage dish. Cover and refrigerate until time to reheat.

Let sauce cool slightly, then strain through a fine sieve into a large nonmetal bowl. Stir in Worcestershire sauce. Cover and refrigerate until fat congeals and rises to the surface. Remove fat.

Sauté mushrooms in butter for 5 minutes. Set aside until ready to use.

Boil onions in salted water until just tender. Drain and set aside until ready to use.

Return sauce and meat to saucepan, add mushrooms and onions. Place over medium flame until thoroughly heated. Add crisp salt pork cubes just before serving.

Serves 6 to 8.

BAROQUE

14 East 53rd Street   *EL 5-4195*

Elegant, small and quiet with supremely deft, unobtrusive service. This is a favorite of connoisseurs of fine French cuisine.

Even the dogs in New York do their share of carrying home the packages. This French poodle lends his mistress a hand on Second Avenue in the Seventies, in the Hungarian section.

Baroque serves lunch from noon to 3:00 P.M. and dinner from 6:00 P.M. to 10:00 P.M. On Saturday dinner only is served, from 5:30 P.M. to 11:00 P.M. Closed Sunday.

STRAWBERRIES ROMANOFF

1½ pints fresh strawberries
1 whole orange
6 teaspoons powdered sugar
2 glasses sweet port wine
3 cups vanilla ice cream
1 cup whipped cream

Hull strawberries and wash thoroughly. Add grated orange peel to strawberries, with sugar and port wine. Let strawberries soak for short time in port wine, then strain off any excess wine. Mix soaked strawberries with slightly softened ice cream. Place in bowl and cover with whipped cream.
Serves 6.

SUPREME OF CHICKEN BAROQUE WITH SAUTÉED NOODLES

6 breasts of chicken, split and boned
4 teaspoons butter
½ carrot, scraped and sliced
½ onion, peeled and chopped
1 cup dry white wine
¼ teaspoon salt
¼ teaspoon pepper
1½ tablespoons flour
1½ cups light cream
½ cup hollandaise sauce (see recipe page 96)
½ cup whipped cream
2 tablespoons freshly grated Parmesan cheese
   Sautéed noodles (see recipe below)
12 asparagus stalks, home-cooked or canned
6 slices *pâté de foie gras*

Brown chicken in butter in heavy sauté pan. Add carrots and onion and cook briefly to brown lightly. Add wine, salt and pepper, cover and cook over medium heat until chicken is tender, about 8 to 10 minutes. Mix the flour with a little of the cream to form a smooth paste; add to sauce and blend well. Remove from heat and discard vegetables. Stir in hollandaise, whipped cream and Parmesan cheese.

Arrange noodles in individual ovenproof molds, top with breast of chicken, slice of *foie gras,* then with 2 asparagus stalks. Pour sauce over each serving and place in preheated 350° F. oven for 5 to 10 minutes to heat thoroughly.

Serves 6.

Sautéed Noodles

1	16-ounce package noodles
¼	teaspoon salt
	Water
3	tablespoons butter

Cook noodles in boiling salted water (according to package directions) until tender. Drain thoroughly, then sauté in melted butter for 3 to 4 minutes.

A LA FOURCHETTE

342 West 46th Street   *CI 5-9744*

For forty-five years this small French restaurant has preserved its intimate clublike ambience and its heritage of Provence. The cuisine is country French, and the specialties of the day are chalked on a big blackboard for the convenience of diner and waiter alike.

À La Fourchette serves lunch from noon to 3:00 P.M. and dinner from 5:00 P.M. to 10:30 P.M. No lunch is served on Saturday. Closed Sundays and the month of August.

CHICKEN BARCELONETTE

2	1½-pound chickens
3	tablespoons butter
1	cup finely chopped cooked spinach
1	egg, lightly beaten
¼	teaspoon salt

Times Square at night, looking north.

¼ teaspoon freshly ground black pepper
¼ teaspoon nutmeg
1 cup Chablis
½ cup light cream
  Boiled noodles

Have butcher bone chicken, remove breasts, split and pound flat. Cut remaining meat of chicken from bone and chop very fine; reserve. Sauté chicken breasts in butter until lightly brown. Spread flat on warm platter and stuff with the following mixture. Combine chopped meat, beaten egg, chopped spinach and seasoning. Blend well. Place a spoonful of stuffing on each breast and roll up. Pack chicken rolls tightly, seam side down, in a small, deep casserole. Add Chablis and cream. Cover casserole tightly and bake in a preheated 350° F. oven for 30 to 35 minutes or until chicken is tender. Remove rolls to a hot plate and cook liquid in pan until it is reduced to half. Pack cooked noodles into individual ovenproof dishes, top with chicken roll, cover with sauce and return to oven for 10 minutes to brown lightly. Serve at once.
Serves 4.

MOULES MARINIÈRES
(Mussels in White Wine)

3 quarts mussels
2 cups dry white wine
6 shallots, finely chopped
5 tablespoons butter
2 tablespoons flour
1 tablespoon parsley, finely chopped
  Salt

Scrub the mussels well, place in a saucepan with the wine and the shallots. Cover and cook over high heat 6 to 8 minutes, or until the shells open. Remove the mussels from the saucepan, reserve the cooking liquid, and take off one shell from each mussel. Place the mussels in a large heated platter and cover with a towel to keep warm.
Cream the butter and flour together into a soft ball and add

to cooking liquid. Boil rapidly until the sauce is reduced by half and is slightly thickened. Add parsley and check for seasoning. Add salt if desired. Pour the sauce over the mussels and serve immediately in deep soup plate. The mussels are eaten directly from the shells.

Serves 6.

CHEZ NAPOLEON

365 West 50th Street   *CO 5-6980*

Theo and Yvette Le Guelaff keep Chez Napoleon small and charming: Theo is the chef; Yvette greets the loyal clientele like old friends. Cuisine is country French but with a highly personal touch.

Chez Napoleon serves lunch from noon to 2:30 P.M. and dinner from 5:00 P.M. to 10:30 P.M. No lunch is served on Saturday. Closed Sunday.

POITRINE DE VOLAILLE A L'ESTRAGON

6	chicken breasts, split, boned and skinned
3	tablespoons flour
1	egg, lightly beaten
½	cup fresh bread crumbs
3	tablespoons butter
6	shallots, chopped
6	chicken livers, chopped
2	tablespoons butter
½	cup dry white wine
2	teaspoons chopped fresh tarragon
1	cup sauce español (brown sauce)

Preheat oven to 400° F.

Pound chicken breast flat, dip first in flour, then in beaten egg, finally in bread crumbs. Place on flat dish and refrigerate until ready to cook.

Melt the 3 tablespoons of butter in a heavy sauté pan and sauté the shallots and chicken livers until tender. Place a teaspoon of the liver-shallot mixture on each chicken breast and roll up jelly-roll fashion. Place in a heavy, deep ovenproof casserole. Melt the 2 tablespoons of butter and pour over chicken rolls and brown in oven.

Combine white wine, tarragon and sauce español in saucepan. Cook over medium heat until reduced by ⅓, about 15 minutes. Pour over browned chicken rolls, cover and bake for 20 to 25 minutes or until chicken is tender. Baste occasionally.

Serves 6.

CAFE BRITTANY

807 Ninth Avenue   *CI 7-9566*

Lively, noisy and fun—here is a true French bistro; good food, fast service and low prices.

Open for lunch from noon to 2:45 P.M. and for dinner from 6:00 P.M. to 10:00 P.M. On Friday and Saturday dinner is served until 11:00 P.M. Closed July.

BOEUF BOURGUIGNON
(Beef in Burgundy Wine)

⅓	pound salt pork, blanched
2	tablespoons butter
24	very small white onions, peeled
2½	pounds boneless chuck, cut into 2-inch pieces (room temperature)
	Salad oil as needed
3	tablespoons flour
½	cup chopped green onion
2	carrots, chopped
3	tablespoons coarsely chopped parsley
½	cup coarsely chopped celery
2	cloves garlic, minced
½	teaspoon pepper
3	cups French Burgundy
2	tablespoons butter
1	cup beef stock
½	pound fresh mushrooms

New Yorker relaxing on a sunny afternoon by watching the cars go by on the Henry Hudson Parkway.

Preheat oven to 350° F.

Cut the pork into small pieces. In a deep, heavy skillet melt the butter and add the pork. Cook over low heat until it is crisp and lightly browned. Drain on paper towels. In the remaining fat brown the onions as evenly as possible; transfer to deep, heavy casserole.

Heat fat to almost smoking, add a little salad oil if needed, and brown the meat as quickly as possible—a few pieces at a time. Transfer meat to casserole as it is browned. When all the meat is in the casserole, sprinkle meat and onion lightly with flour, turning to coat evenly. Cook over medium heat for about 10 minutes to brown flour, stirring constantly to prevent burning. Add the green onion, carrots, parsley, celery, garlic, pepper, Burgundy, stock and pork bits. Cover and place casserole in oven and bake at 350° F. for 2 to 2½ hours or until meat is tender and sauce has thickened.

Just before cooking is completed melt the 2 tablespoons of butter and sauté the mushrooms in it until barely tender. Add to casserole and cook a final 15 minutes. Allow casserole to cool slightly to thicken before serving.

Serves 6.

BRITTANY DU SOIR

800 Ninth Avenue   *CO 5-4820*

A "Breton country inn" is the way owner Gilbert Seveneante describes his beamed-ceiling restaurant. Seveneante is from Brittany, of course, but even more important so is his chef.

Brittany du Soir serves lunch from noon to 2:45 P.M. and dinner from 5:00 P.M. to 11:15 P.M. Closed Sunday and August (when the entire staff goes home to Brittany).

VEAL MARENGO

3   pounds boneless veal, cut into 2-inch pieces
4   tablespoons salad oil
2   tablespoons butter

½	cup finely chopped onions
½	cup finely chopped shallots
3	tablespoons flour
¼	teaspoon salt
½	teaspoon pepper
¾	cup dry white wine
2	cups beef stock
2	whole tomatoes, chopped
4	tablespoons parsley, chopped
1	bay leaf
3	tablespoons butter
12	tiny white onions, peeled
42	whole fresh mushrooms

Preheat oven to 450° F. Brown the pieces of veal in the oil in a large, heavy skillet. Brown only a few pieces at a time—the oil should be very hot to sear the meat quickly. Add more oil if needed.

Transfer the browned meat to a heavy, deep oven casserole. Pour off unused oil in skillet and wipe with paper towels. Melt the butter in the skillet and sauté the onions and shallots over low heat until limp and slightly browned.

Sprinkle the meat into the casserole with flour, salt and pepper; turn with a fork until meat is well coated with seasoned flour. Place casserole in preheated oven (uncovered) and bake for about 10 minutes until well browned and all trace of white flour has disappeared. Turn frequently.

Remove casserole from oven and lower heat to 325° F. Add sautéed onion and shallots, the wine, stock, chopped tomatoes, parsley and bay leaf. Cover and return casserole to oven and bake for 1½ to 2 hours or until veal is tender and sauce has thickened. About ½ hour before veal is completely cooked, melt the 3 tablespoons of butter in the skillet and in it sauté the onions until golden brown but still crisp. Add to veal mixture. Repeat the process with the mushrooms, adding them to the casserole about 15 minutes before removing from the oven. Let the stew cool slightly to thicken before serving.

Serves 6.

CAFÉ DE FRANCE

330 West 46th Street   *CO 5-8927*

The chef and part owner is from Burgundy and, naturally, so is the cuisine. Small and pleasant with excellent service against a background of gastronomic maps of France.

Café de France serves lunch from noon to 3:00 P.M. and dinner from 5:00 P.M. to 10:30 P.M. On Friday and Saturday dinner is served until 11:30 P.M. Closed Sunday.

POUSSIN RÔTI CAFÉ DE FRANCE

6	whole squab, cleaned and dressed
2	teaspoons salt
2	teaspoons pepper
3	tablespoons butter
3	teaspoons mustard
1	teaspoon thyme
1	tablespoon salad oil
¼	cup white wine
2	tablespoons Cognac
½	cup light cream
½	cup chicken stock

Preheat oven to 450° F. Rub squab inside and out with a mixture of the salt, pepper and butter. Place in oven on a rack in deep roasting pan. Roast for 15 to 20 minutes. Blend mustard, thyme, salad oil and wine. Remove squab from oven and baste well with wine mixture. Return to oven for 10 to 15 minutes. Transfer squab to heated platter. Skim fat from liquid left in roasting pan. Add Cognac, cream and chicken stock. Cook over low heat until sauce has thickened. Do not allow to boil. To serve, cut squab in two, top with hot sauce. Serve with parsleyed new potatoes and sautéed mushrooms.

Serves 6.

LA PETITE FERME

189 West 10th Street   *242-7035*

One of the most charming and best restaurants in New York.
So small that its rough white plaster walls will accommodate at
one time only twenty diners at its pine tables with their ladder-
back chairs—but what matter? The food is the star: wonderfully
simple bourgeois food prepared by owner Charles Chevillot, who
is, not so incidentally, a son of the family who owns the famous
Hotel de la Poste in Beaune, France.

La Petite Ferme serves lunch from noon to 3:00 P.M. and dinner from 6:00 P.M. to 11:00 P.M. Closed Monday.

POULE AU POT
(Chicken Broth)

4	quarts cold water
1	small cabbage cut into large pieces
3	or 4 leeks cut into 2-inch pieces
4	turnips cut in half and washed but *not* peeled
2	or 3 celery ribs
4	carrots, washed but *not* peeled
¼	teaspoon salt
½	teaspoon freshly ground black pepper
2	bay leaves
½	teaspoon cloves
3	small onions, whole, *not* peeled
½	teaspoon basil

Put all ingredients in a large soup kettle and allow to come to
a full boil. Lower heat and let simmer for 1 hour.

Poule
(Chicken for the Pot)

1	2½- to 3-pound chicken with liver and gizzard
¾	cup fresh bread crumbs
¾	cup parsley
½	pound cooked ham, finely chopped
2	eggs

One of the tiniest restaurants in New York, in Greenwich Village, owned and operated by Charles Chevillot, a great French chef widely known for his cooking style.

1   clove garlic
1   tablespoon butter, melted
¼   teaspoon salt

Wash chicken inside and out and pat dry. Chop liver and gizzard. Discard neck. Mix chicken liver and gizzard with bread crumbs, parsley, chopped ham, eggs, garlic, butter and salt. Blend well.

Stuff chicken loosely with mixture and tie wings and legs to body with butcher's string. Close cavity by sewing together with darning needle and white cotton thread. Place chicken in simmering broth and cook uncovered over low heat for 2 to 2½ hours. When chicken is tender remove from broth, let cool slightly, cut into serving portions and serve in soup plates with a generous helping of broth for each serving. Serve with French bread.

Serves 4 to 6.

PIERRE AU TUNNEL

306 West 48th Street   *CO 5-9039*

The restaurant is tunnel-shaped and the owner is Pierre Pujol: what else to call the restaurant but Pierre au Tunnel? But regardless of the name, here is a find: unpretentious but excellent French fare at very attractive prices.

The restaurant serves lunch from noon to 3:00 P.M. and dinner from 5:30 to 11:30 P.M. Closed Sunday.

TRIPE A LA MODE DE CAEN

4   large onions, peeled and chopped
4   large carrots, scraped and chopped
4   pounds plain beef tripe, cut into 2-inch squares
1   calf's foot, split
4   leeks, tied together
4   cloves garlic, peeled
1   teaspoon salt
¼   teaspoon pepper

1 cup dry white wine
½ cup Calvados
   Bouquet garni of
      2 ribs celery
      2 sprigs parsley
      2 bay leaves
      1 sprig thyme
½ pound beef suet
16 small potatoes, boiled and peeled

Spread onions and carrots over the bottom of a large oven-proof casserole (one that may also be used on the top of the stove), cover with tripe and add remaining ingredients except beef suet.

Cut suet into slices about ½ inch thick and lay them on top of casserole so that the entire surface is covered. Pour in just enough water to come to the top of the ingredients. Cover casserole and bring to a full boil on top of stove. Then place in preheated 300° F. oven and let cook for 8 to 10 hours. Remove calf's foot and cut meat from bone. Discard bone and cut meat into pieces about the same size as tripe. Strain liquid and refrigerate until fat has risen to the surface and congealed. Remove and discard fat.

To serve, place portions of the tripe and calf's foot in 8 individual casseroles. Pour strained and skimmed liquid over them. Place in a preheated 425° F. oven until thoroughly heated. Place 2 very hot boiled potatoes in each casserole and serve at once.

Serves 8.

PÂTÉ MAISON

1 pound pork liver
2 pounds lean pork
¾ pound pork fat
4 chicken livers
2 teaspoons salt
¼ teaspoon pepper
¼ teaspoon thyme
½ teaspoon sage

¾ cup dry sherry
¼ cup Cognac
2 bay leaves

Grind together pork liver, lean pork, pork fat and chicken livers, using fine blade of grinder. Add salt, pepper, thyme, sage, sherry and Cognac. Mix thoroughly. Turn into 2½-quart earthenware casserole which has been well greased on the bottom. Top with bay leaves. Cover. Bake at 350° F. for 1½ hours. Uncover and bake 20 minutes longer. Chill thoroughly before serving.

Serves 10 to 12 as an appetizer.

CASSOULET TAULORESAIN

3 cups dried white beans
½ teaspoon salt
½ pound garlic sausage
3 ounces fat salt pork, cut into small cubes
2 pounds shoulder of lamb, cut into 1½-inch cubes
2½ pounds duck, cut into small serving pieces
Salt
Pepper
2 medium onions, peeled, finely chopped
2 cloves garlic, peeled and minced
Bouquet garni of
3 sprigs parsley
2 ribs celery
½ bay leaf
3 sprigs thyme
all tied together in small bunch

In a large pot soak beans in cold water to cover for 4 hours. Bring to a full boil, then remove from heat and drain. Cover with fresh cold water, add the ½ teaspoon of salt and the sausage and let simmer for 35 minutes. Remove sausage and set aside. Cook beans for an additional 25 minutes.

Place salt pork cubes in a saucepan with water to cover and bring to boil. Lower heat and let simmer for 5 minutes. Drain and pat thoroughly dry with paper toweling. Place in a large saucepan and cook over low heat until cubes are crisp and all fat has been rendered. Remove pork with a slotted spoon and set aside. Heat fat to almost smoking and add pieces of lamb and duck, a few at a time, turning them as they cook until well browned on all sides. When all meat has been browned, lower heat, add onions and garlic, cook briefly just until soft, sprinkle lightly with salt and pepper and add to the pan just enough water to cover. Bring to a boil, add garlic, *bouquet garni,* and reserved crisp salt pork cubes. Lower heat and let simmer for 30 minutes. Taste and add more salt if desired. Drain and add beans. Cover pan and let simmer over low heat for 1½ to 2 hours, or until meat and beans are tender. Remove and discard *bouquet garni.* Cool slightly, then refrigerate until fat has risen to the surface. Remove and discard fat.

To serve rub the inside of 5 or 6 individual ovenproof casseroles with a split clove of garlic. Into each casserole place some of the lamb and the duck. Cover with beans and top with slices of sausage and salt pork. Place in a preheated 400° F. oven for 15 to 20 minutes or until well heated. Serve in casseroles.

Serves 5 to 6.

RENÉ PUJOL RESTAURANT

321 West 51st Street   *246-3023*

Brick walls, gleaming copper pots and pans and a beamed ceiling make this "French Country Inn" a pleasant background for the specialties of the French Pyrenees. Deft service, and a very personal touch created by owner Rene Pujol.

Lunch is served from noon to 3:00 P.M. and dinner from 5:00 P.M. to 11:00 P.M. Closed Sunday.

SCAMPI AMANDINE

4 shallots, peeled and finely chopped
1 cup dry white wine
½ pound butter
½ cup finely grated almonds
½ cup fine dry bread crumbs
3 egg yolks

        Salt
        Pepper
30   jumbo shrimp
½   cup dry vermouth
        Slivered almonds

Place shallots in ½ cup of the wine in a small saucepan. Let simmer over low heat until wine has evaporated.

Refrigerate 2 tablespoons of the butter. Bring remaining butter to room temperature.

Combine onions, room-temperature butter, grated almonds, bread crumbs and egg yolks. Blend until mixture is smooth and then season lightly with salt and pepper.

Peel and devein shrimp, leaving the tail attached. Split down the inside lengthwise, being careful not to cut through the shrimp. Spread open. Spoon some of the prepared almond-butter mixture onto each shrimp, spreading it out to cover shrimp completely.

Place shrimp in single layer in a well-buttered shallow baking pan. Top each with slivers of the reserved cold butter and with almond slivers. Pour vermouth and remaining white wine around them. Place in a preheated 350° F. oven and bake for 15 minutes. Serve at once.

Serves 6.

The internationally known Peacock Alley off the Waldorf-Astoria lobby, where through the years New Yorkers and visitors alike have

come to see and be seen.

Chapter II

ITALIAN FOOD

~~~~~~

Restaurants and Recipes

DURING the height of the immigration wave at the turn of the century, Italians poured into the United States by the millions. Most of those who stayed in New York settled in neighborhoods with people from their own villages. They quickly set about re-creating the world they had left behind. They brought with them their own kind of cooking, their own foods, even the apparatus to make their own wines. In these neighborhoods English was the foreign language.

The best known of the neighborhoods was the southern part of Greenwich Village and the traditional "Little Italy" of the Lower East Side from Canal to Bleecker Streets between Broadway and the Bowery.

Beginning in the 1920s, some of the new generations began to move to other parts of the city, spreading the culture and the cuisine of Italy. Today there are Italian restaurants in every part of the city; the most elegant, the most chic and the best are in midtown Manhattan. They offer a taste of the good life of Rome, Florence and Milan.

But the old Italian neighborhoods continue. Unlike some

foreign groups who moved northward, all but abandoning their old neighborhoods to newer immigrant groups, the Italians have stayed. Almost 40 percent of the more than one million Italians now in New York continue to live in the same neighborhoods as their parents did.

In these neighborhoods Italians, the second largest ethnic group in the city, are able to preserve to a large degree the cultural style of the Old World village. The restaurants are here, the markets, the cafés. During the Festa of San Gennaro, the week of September 19, the streets of Little Italy blaze to life. And at the first sign of spring the men emerge from the long winter for the season's first game of bocci ball.

THE FOODS OF ITALY

What a shame that so many people think only of pasta when they think of Italian food. Pasta is to Southern Italians what rice is to the Orientals and potatoes are to the Irish, but this is only a small part of the story. The food of Italy is as varied as the country itself.

Until recently Italy was a medley of small provinces each with its own traditions, cuisine and people. The Milanese use rice as frequently as pasta, while the rich tomato and cheese sauce of the Romans is rare; and though olive oil is part of almost every Italian recipe, the Northern Italian cook will often substitute butter.

Florence, heart of what was the province of Tuscany, is famous for chicken and meat, particularly steak, and for a fairly sophisticated cuisine. After all, it was Tuscan-born Catherine de Medici who introduced civilized food to France when she brought her own chefs to the French court. And while the Romans do love their pasta, it is served in a far more delicate way than the robust and spicily sauced version of the Siciliano.

Cheese, from the very mild and bland to the pungent and sharp, is part and parcel of Italian cuisine, and all of Italy loves its spices and herbs. Basil, oregano, peppers (both sweet and hot), a lavish use of parsley, onions, shallots and garlic are typi-

On Mulberry Street in Little Italy, a corner store filled with lots of

Italian delicacies.

cal, but the Northern Italian cook will strive for a nuance of flavor while his Southern cousin seasons with a bolder hand.

Cooking methods range from the slow-cooking sauce to quickly broiled meats and fish, so it is impossible to say one type of dish is typically "Italian"; the food is too varied and too interesting. Generally speaking, however, Italian food has more "gusto" than the more subtly flavored food of France. Typically Italian menus follow a set pattern: antipasto, then pasta, followed by meat or fish, salad or cold cooked vegetables, cheese and usually fruit. Then finally, espresso, more espresso and talk, for good conversation is an intregal part of every Italian meal. Wine, of course, always wine; even in bustling, money-minded Milan there's wine for lunch.

To savor the best of Italian cooking in this country, do as the Italians. Find an Italian grocer who imports their superb long-grain rice, who has crusty Italian-type bread, who has fresh real Italian cheeses, especially Bel Paese, Gorgonzola, homemade mozzarella and, above all, real, honest-to-goodness Parmesan that you grate yourself. Italian tomatoes, the best in the world, can be had in jars and cans, and, best of all, real Italian pasta made from the finest durum wheat is available in Italian specialty shops.

In brief, Italian cooking is relaxed, easy and simple; it is the combination of superb ingredients that makes it one of the most enjoyable cuisines in the world.

SAN MARCO

52 West 55th Street   *CI 6-5340*

San Marco, which takes its name from the piazza in Venice and its menu from the North of Italy, may just be the best Italian restaurant in town. A small, tastefully furnished dining room with 25 tables at most, San Marco offers gracious service, a cozy, intimate atmosphere and, above all, excellent food. Its Northern Italian dishes, lighter and less spicy than their Southern relatives, are cooked to order; none is prepared in advance.

Bottles of Italian wine are part of the decor in the Marbona on Grand Street, near Mulberry Street, the Italian section of lower Manhattan.

San Marco serves lunch from noon to 3:00 P.M. and dinner from 5:30 P.M. to 10:30 P.M. Closed Sunday.

LASAGNE ALLA NAPOLIANA

1	pound lasagne (flat Italian noodles)
½	teaspoon salt
2	tablespoons softened butter
2	cups Neapolitan meat sauce (see below)
½	pound mozzarella cheese, thinly sliced
½	cup grated Parmesan cheese
3	tablespoons butter, cut into slivers
3	tablespoons chopped parsley

Cook lasagne according to package directions in boiling salted water until just barely *al dente;* do not overcook. Drain well and mix with the softened butter. Butter a 2-quart baking dish and place one layer of the drained lasagne in the bottom, cover with a layer of mozzarella, a layer of Parmesan, then with a layer of sauce; repeat until all ingredients are used, topping with a layer of lasagne. Dot this with the 3 tablespoons of butter and bake in a preheated moderate oven (325° F.) for 30 to 40 minutes until it is bubbling hot. Sprinkle each serving generously with parsley.

Serves 4–6.

Neapolitan Meat Sauce

3	tablespoons olive oil
1	small onion, chopped
½	pound lean chopped beef
6	tomatoes, seeded and chopped
¼	teaspoon salt
¼	teaspoon pepper

Heat the oil in a deep, heavy skillet; sauté the onion until just limp; add meat and cook over medium heat until well browned, stirring frequently to break up into small particles. Add tomatoes and salt and pepper, lower heat and simmer slowly until sauce is smooth and thick. May be used at once or made ahead of time and refrigerated or frozen until ready to use.

On Mulberry Street these little girls in their new Easter clothes have just bought a bag of Italian olives as a snack to munch on.

CHICKEN CASORZO

- 8   chicken breasts, boned and skinned
- 2   tablespoons flour
- ½   teaspoon salt
- ½   teaspoon pepper
- 2   tablespoons olive oil
- 3   tablespoons butter
- 1   green pepper, seeded and sliced into strips
- ½   red pepper, seeded and sliced into strips
- ½   pound fresh mushrooms
- 2   ripe tomatoes, peeled, seeded and chopped
- 1   tablespoon tomato paste
- 1   cup dry red wine
-    Parsley

Roll chicken breasts in a mixture of the flour, salt and pepper; heat oil and butter in a deep, heavy sauté pan. Brown the chicken breasts. Remove to a heated platter and keep warm.

Sauté the peppers and mushrooms in the remaining fat until peppers are soft and mushrooms lightly brown, adding more butter if necessary. Pour off excess fat, return chicken breasts to pan, add chopped tomatoes, tomato paste and wine. Cover and cook over low heat for 10 to 15 minutes or until chicken is tender. Remove chicken to heated serving dish and thicken sauce by cooking over high heat 5 to 10 minutes. Pour over chicken, garnish with parsley and serve.

Serves 4.

MARCHI'S

251 East 31st Street   *OR 9-2494*

One of the handsomest restaurants in town, Marchi's is housed in a lovely old townhouse on a pretty tree-lined street. Very much like dining at a private house, there is no sign outside, and no printed menu. Tables are set with fresh flowers and candles and the food is Italian at its very best.

Marchi's serves dinner only. Open 5:30 to 10:00 P.M. Closed Sundays.

LASAGNE MARCHI

2   cups lean ground beef
3   eggs, lightly beaten
1   clove garlic, minced
2   tablespoons freshly grated Parmesan cheese
1   tablespoon olive oil (more if needed)
3   tablespoons butter
1   whole clove garlic, peeled
2   very ripe tomatoes, cut into chunks
2   tablespoons Italian tomato paste
1   bay leaf
¼   teaspoon salt
¼   teaspoon freshly grated black pepper
½   pound Italian sausage cut into thin slices
1   pound lasagne (broad flat noodles)
½   pound mozzarella cheese, cut into thin slices
½   pound ricotta cheese
½   cup freshly grated Parmesan cheese

Combine beef, eggs, minced garlic and the 2 tablespoons of Parmesan cheese. Form into small meatballs. Heat the olive oil and 2 tablespoons of the butter in a deep, heavy sauté pan with the whole clove of garlic. Remove garlic when it starts to brown. Brown meatballs in the garlic-flavored oil-butter mixture. Add a little extra oil if necessary. When meatballs are evenly browned, pour off excess oil and add tomatoes, tomato paste, bay leaf, salt and pepper; lower heat and allow to simmer for 30 to 45 minutes. Sauté Italian sausage slices in remaining butter and set aside. Cook lasagne according to package directions in rapidly boiling salted water *al dente* (tender but still firm).

Remove bay leaf and pour about ¼ of the tomato sauce into a fairly deep ovenproof casserole. Over it arrange a layer of noodles, one slice of mozzarella, a layer of sausage and one of meatballs; spread ricotta cheese over meat, sprinkle generously with grated Parmesan and finish with a layer of sauce. Repeat the layers until all the ingredients have been used. Finish with a sprinkling of Parmesan. Bake at 300° F. for 25 minutes.

Serves 6.

For the best Italian cheeses and olive oil, try Alleva on Mulberry Street.

CREME FRITTA
(Fried Tartlet with Creme Filling)

2 cups flour
2 teaspoons baking powder
¼ teaspoon salt
2 tablespoons sugar
4 tablespoons lukewarm water
3 tablespoons butter
1 teaspoon vanilla
1 egg
2 tablespoons Marsala wine
Peanut oil
Creme filling (see below)

Sift together flour, baking powder and salt. Dissolve sugar in lukewarm water. Blend butter into flour mixture, add egg and blend well. Add water-sugar and wine; blend. Knead until smooth on lightly floured board. Place in bowl and refrigerate for one hour.

Roll out to ⅛-inch thickness and cut into rounds about 3 inches in diameter. Fill a deep kettle with oil to 2 inches of rim and heat to 375° F. on a deep-frying thermometer. Fry rounds 1 minute or until lightly browned. Drain on paper towels and allow to cool. When completely cooled, spread each disk with creme filling and top with another disk to form a tartlet. Refrigerate until ready to serve. Dust with powdered sugar before serving.

Creme Filling

1 pound ricotta cheese
1 square bitter chocolate, melted and cooled
1 tablespoon chopped citron
1 teaspoon almond flavor
4 tablespoons sugar
2 tablespoons grated orange rind
1 tablespoon grated lemon rind

Combine all ingredients and blend in an electric blender until smooth and "custardy." Refrigerate until ready to use. An electric mixer may be used instead of a blender but the creme will not be so smooth.

Makes about 2 dozen.

The United Nations buildings and the promenade facing the East River.

PAOLUCCI'S

149 Mulberry Street   *226-9653*

Run by the same Italian family for years, Paolucci's has a loyal following who dote on the hearty informality, as well as the equally hearty Neapolitan cooking.

Exceptional pasta and the fresh-daily tomato sauce are well worth the trip downtown.

Paolucci's is open from 12:00 noon to 11:00 P.M. seven days a week.

ARAGOSTA FRA DIAVOLO

(Lobster with Tomatoes and Red Peppers)

2	live lobsters, about 1½ pounds each
1	tablespoon olive oil
1	tablespoon butter
1	clove garlic, peeled and chopped
2	large tomatoes, peeled, seeded and chopped
3	tablespoons chopped parsley
1	teaspoon oregano
¼	teaspoon crushed red-pepper seeds
⅛	teaspoon salt
⅛	teaspoon pepper
2	tablespoons grated Parmesan cheese

With a very sharp knife, split spinal cord of the lobster by inserting between body and tail. Split open. Remove small sac just back of the head. The coral is edible and delicious so retain it for extra flavor. Place lobsters, cut side up, in large baking dish. Set aside.

Heat olive oil and butter in heavy skillet and sauté garlic until soft and transparent; add rest of ingredients, except cheese, and simmer over low heat for 15 minutes or until blended into a thick sauce. Pour over lobster and bake in a 350° F. oven for about 20 minutes or until lobster is tender. Sprinkle with grated Parmesan cheese and return to oven until cheese is melted (about 3 minutes).

Serves 4.

ROTOLINI A LA MARSALA

1	pound rump of veal, thinly sliced
½	pound prosciutto, finely minced
1	clove garlic, minced
1	large onion, finely minced
2	tablespoons chopped parsley
¼	teaspoon salt
¼	teaspoon pepper
2	tablespoons olive oil
2	tablespoons butter
2	large tomatoes, peeled, seeded and chopped
1	tablespoon tomato paste
½	cup Marsala wine
8	whole mushrooms
2	tablespoons butter
	Salt
	Pepper

Have butcher slice veal as thinly as possible, then pound out to wafer thin. Combine minced prosciutto, garlic, onion, chopped parsley, salt and pepper. Blend. Place a tablespoon of mixture on each slice of veal and roll up carefully, tucking ends inside. Tie with butcher's white string. Heat oil and butter in deep, heavy sauté pan and brown meat rolls over medium-high heat, turning carefully. Pour off excess fat; add tomatoes, tomato paste and Marsala. Cover and cook over low heat for 30 to 45 minutes or until rolls are tender. Heat butter in a small skillet and sauté mushrooms. Add to meat dish just before serving. Correct seasoning with salt and pepper as needed.

Serves 6.

GROTTA AZZURRA INN

387 Broome Street 226-9283

The Grotta Azzurra (Blue Grotto) is a dimly lit, pleasant restaurant hung with Italian paintings; of course there is an overall blue decor.

A long-time favorite with Italian food fans, it is usually crowded, so reservations are in order. The pasta is cooked strictly to order, so plan for a leisurely meal.

Grotta Azzurra is open from 11:30 A.M. to midnight. Closed on Mondays and the last three weeks in July.

MERLUZZO GROTTA AZZURRA

(Whiting in Tomato Sauce)

2	pounds whiting
2	tablespoons olive oil
2	tablespoons butter
1	small onion, peeled and minced
1	clove garlic, peeled and minced
1	carrot, scraped and finely diced
2	tablespoons chopped parsley
2	large tomatoes, peeled, seeded and diced
1	tablespoon tomato paste
½	cup Soave (dry white wine)
⅛	teaspoon salt
⅛	teaspoon pepper

Have fish cleaned. Wash carefully and pat dry with paper towels. Cut crosswise into serving-size pieces. Refrigerate while sauce is being made.

Heat olive oil and butter; sauté minced onion and garlic until soft but not brown. Add carrot, parsley, tomatoes, wine and seasoning. Simmer slowly over low heat for 25 to 30 minutes until sauce blends and thickens. Place fish in deep nonmetal baking dish, pour sauce over fish, cover and bake in 300° F. oven 20 to 25 minutes or until fish flakes easily with a fork. Serve very hot.

Serves 4.

FRITTOMISTO

(Assorted Fried Vegetables)

Batter

½	cup flour
⅛	teaspoon salt

½	teaspoon sugar
2	eggs
¼	cup milk
1	tablespoon butter, melted and cooled

Vegetables

4	zucchini, in 1-inch slices
1	head cauliflower, broken into 1-inch flowerettes
2	large green peppers, seeded and cut into 1-inch-wide strips
1	small eggplant, peeled and cut into 1-inch cubes
½	cup flour
1	teaspoon salt
	Vegetable oil for frying

Sift flour, salt and sugar into mixing bowl. Beat eggs and milk together; add melted butter and stir into flour mixture. Blend well and refrigerate for 30 minutes while you prepare vegetables.

Plunge zucchini slices, cauliflower flowerettes and pepper strips into briskly boiling water and cook over high heat for 3 minutes. Remove with sieve or slotted spoon and drain. Do not blanch eggplant. Combine flour and salt, and roll vegetables in it until well coated. Heat enough oil in a heavy, deep pot to hold vegetables without crowding. Dip floured vegetable pieces into chilled batter and drop immediately into hot oil, a few at a time. Fry until delicately browned. Drain on paper towels and serve hot.

Serves 4 to 6.

GRANITA DI LIMONE

(Italian Lemon Ice)

4	cups water
2	cups sugar
1	tablespoon grated lemon rind
1	cup lemon juice
½	cup sugar
3	tablespoons water
⅛	teaspoon cream of tartar
1	egg white, stiffly beaten
1	tablespoon Strega

Combine water and sugar. Bring to a boil and boil for 5 minutes. Cool and add grated lemon rind and juice. Freeze in ice-cube trays to mushy stage.

About 2 hours before serving, dissolve the ½ cup of sugar in the 3 tablespoons of water; add cream of tartar. Boil over high heat without stirring until the syrup spins a thread or reaches 270° F. on a candy thermometer. Pour the syrup slowly into the stiffly beaten egg white, beating constantly as you pour. Continue to beat with a rotary beater until meringue is very thick and completely cooled.

Remove sherbet from ice tray, place in a large mixing bowl and break up with a fork. Quickly blend in meringue mixture and the Strega. Pile into sherbet glass and refreeze until firm. Serves 6.

CAFÉ VERDI

192 Bleecker Street   *473-9146*

Summers in Italy, those cool, dim cafés where the coffee was fresh espresso steamed from a gleaming, hissing machine, and the cake was a rich concoction of creams and fruits and sweet wines.

When Carlo Antonio came to New York in 1957, he missed the cafés of his native Genoa. For a while he worked in some of the grander restaurants. Then he opened Café Verdi, an Italian-style café in Greenwich Village. It is neat and clean, cool and dim, the walls are wood-paneled, the tablecloths are red, the coffee is fresh espresso steamed from a gleaming, hissing machine, and the cake . . .

Café Verdi serves from 11:30 A.M. to 2 A.M.

ZUPPA INGLESE

1	pint milk
5	egg yolks
⅓	cup sugar

All ages are represented in this picture taken in a Greenwich Village coffeehouse. They specialize in glacées at this one, the Café Borgia on Bleecker Street.

⅓	cup flour
1	scant teaspoon cornstarch
½	teaspoon grated lemon rind
2	teaspoons cocoa
1	large (about 12 inches) sponge cake, homemade or from a good bakery
¾	cup Marsala wine
¼	cup sweet vermouth
	Strawberry jam
1	cup heavy cream
2	tablespoons sugar

Combine milk, egg yolks, sugar, flour and cornstarch in electric blender and blend until smooth. Pour into saucepan and place over medium heat; stir in lemon rind. Cook, stirring, until thick. Do not allow to boil. Pour ½ of the custard into a bowl. Add cocoa to remaining ½ and blend well. Refrigerate both custards until cold.

Cut sponge cake into 3 layers and pour Marsala equally over 2 of the layers. Spread them with a thin layer of strawberry jam. Cover 1 layer with lemon-flavored custard, second layer with chocolate custard. Put layers together, top with third layer and pour vermouth over surface. Chill cake.

Whip cream until stiff. Fold in sugar. Use to cover sides and top of cake. Garnish top with strawberry jam.

Serves 8.

TRATTORIA

Main Concourse, Pan Am Building   *MO 1-3090*

This sleek but informal Italian restaurant was inspired by some of the new trattorias in Italy. The wood-paneled room is bright with Italian posters, white settees and striped glass globes designed by Venini.

Trattoria is open from 7:30 A.M. to 2 A.M. On Saturday and Sunday the restaurant opens at noon.

ZABIANI

- 9 egg yolks
- 9 tablespoons sugar
- 12 tablespoons Marsala wine
- 12 ladyfingers

Place all ingredients except ladyfingers in the top half of a double boiler over barely simmering water. Stir and whip with a wire whisk until heavy and thick, about 5 to 10 minutes. Spoon into sherbet glasses. Garnish each glass with 2 ladyfingers and serve warm.

Serves 6.

A vest-pocket children's playground tucked among the old buildings

along Mulberry Street, downtown New York.

Chapter III

SWISS FOOD

~~~~~~

Restaurants and Recipes

THIRTY THOUSAND Swiss, most of them German-speaking, now live in New York, having left behind the snow-capped mountains and green pastures of their tiny country.

What they have brought with them, though, is their famous foods, which combine the French-German-Italian influences on Switzerland. Most of these foods—from fondues, rye bread and tender veal to blueberries grown on mountainsides—can be had in the handful of Swiss restaurants strewn through New York's Forties, both East Side and West.

Along with Switzerland's foods, these restaurants are the places to taste the best of the Swiss wines, some available no-where else—not even in wine shops—in the United States.

Each of these restaurants is a visual delight, a re-creation of a part of the world the Swiss left behind. Switzerland was never closer to New York than in these restaurants.

SWISS CUISINE

One part North Italian, one part French, one part German, Swiss cuisine is a happy blend of the best of all three. Developed into a fine art by the "Nation of Innkeepers" (and they are the best in the world), Swiss cuisine is far more than fondue and cheese.

Because this clean and beautiful country has some of the best dairy products in the world, it follows that cream, eggs, cheese and veal would take a starring role, and indeed they do. The delicately sauced veal dishes, the rich egg custard, onion and cheese pies eaten either hot or cold, and the superbly flavorful thin slices of sautéed veal make for dining that has the delicacy of France with a touch of German heartiness.

Cheese more often than not begins the meal, usually in the form of little cheese tarts with infinite variations: made with ham, mushrooms, bits of chicken, in fact, with whatever the chef may have on hand, all bound together in an airy, light custard of eggs and cream, the whole presented in a flaky pastry shell.

No one surpasses the Swiss chef in the art of preparing fish; both trout and perch abound in Switzerland's crystal-clear lakes and rivers, and the Swiss have raised fish cookery to a fine art. In fact, Swiss cuisine does tend to be a bit elaborate; the finest chefs in the world are Swiss-trained, and who does not like to display his skill just a bit? Fish, in particular, lends itself to delicate sauces and seasonings, and the happy result makes for superb eating.

This same love of skillful preparation is evident in meat dishes as well; not for the Swiss the plain roast of other countries. Veal, the most popular meat, is sauced and creamed, flavored with mushrooms and truffles. Who would complain?

For dessert there is pastry, and what pastry—as delicate as a cloud, usually filled with an almond-flavored cream or glazed fruits enhanced by more than a little kirsch, Switzerland's superb liquor.

One final note on Swiss cuisine: the happy Swiss have perfected the fine art of "snacking." Wonderful sausages and naturally great cheeses, good breads and superb beer are just as much a part of Swiss dining as the more elaborate menus. And who could ignore the fondue? That most convivial of dishes, no one could possibly be lonely or unhappy with a fine group of friends and a superbly made Swiss fondue.

There is good reason that Americans love Switzerland and Swiss food. Certainly no more varied cuisine exists and it is prepared with but one objective in mind—the pleasure of dining well, perhaps better than you have ever dined before.

CHALET SUISSE

6 East 48th Street   *355-0855*

The Chalet Suisse looks like a Swiss chalet with immaculate white walls, red-patterned carpet and, overhead, dark wood beams between rounded arches. It is all neat and pristine, yet comfortable and as appealing as a cozy Swiss ski lodge. Owner Konrad Egli says the decor is typical of restaurants in his native Switzerland. And so is the food, a nice balance of French and German cooking styles.

Some of Switzerland's best wines can be found here.

Chalet Suisse serves lunch from noon to 3:00 P.M. and dinner from 5:00 P.M. to 9:30 P.M. Closed Saturday and Sunday.

DEEP-SEA FONDUE CHALET SUISSE

At serving time heat bouillon in fondue pot and keep at a simmer on a chafing-dish burner at table. Have ready the filets of sole, scallops and lobster pieces. Provide each guest with a portion of each of these seafood bits and two forks: one for the cooking (which gets hot) and one for eating.

Provide each guest with wedges of lemon and a variety of sauces. Each cooks his own seafood, a piece at a time, in the simmering bouillon: 30–45 seconds for the sole, about 1 minute each for the scallop slices, and 1½ minutes for each of the lobster segments. Sauces are for dipping. Bouillon is for sipping at end of meal.

Fish Bouillon

4   cups bottled clam juice
2   cups dry white wine
2   cups water

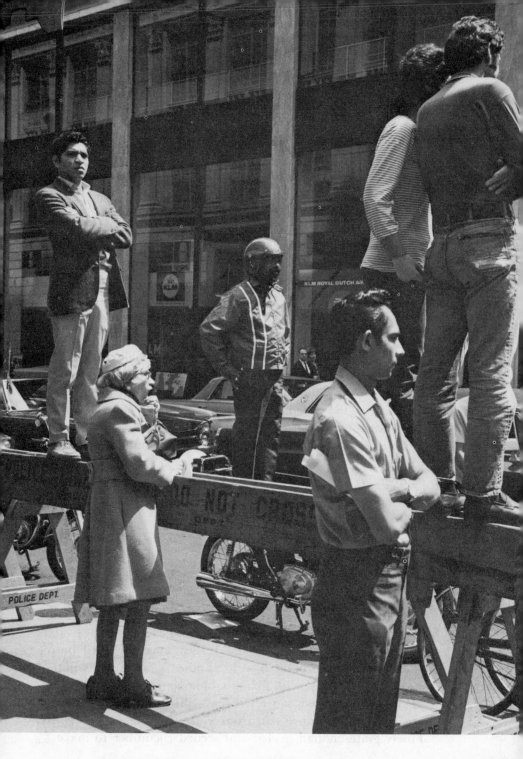

Parade watching on East 49th Street and Fifth Avenue.

1	large onion, peeled and finely chopped
1	large carrot, scraped and finely chopped
1	rib celery, finely chopped
4	peppercorns
1	bay leaf
½	teaspoon salt

Bring liquid to a boil, add remaining ingredients and cook over moderate heat for 30 minutes. Strain bouillon and reserve. Discard solids.

Seafoods for Dunking

1	pound filets of sole, cut into 2-inch lengths
12	large deep-sea scallops, each cut into 3 slices
4	lobster tails, good size, cut into bite-size pieces

SAUCES

Can be ready-made or homemade. At the Chalet Suisse Konrad Egli serves hollandaise, tartar, lobster sauces and lemon wedges with this fondue. When he first served his invention to Alvin Kerr, the noted lecturer and writer for *Gourmet* magazine, Kerr was so delighted with this new fondue that he dreamed up a sauce variation of his own, cucumber-hollandaise, which we give below. For plain hollandaise simply omit cucumber.

Cucumber-Hollandaise Sauce

3	egg yolks
1	teaspoon lemon juice
¼	teaspoon salt
12	tablespoons (1½ sticks) unsalted butter
¼	cup cucumber, peeled, seeded, grated

In top of double boiler combine egg yolks, lemon juice and salt. Set pan over simmering water; immediately add 4 tablespoons unsalted butter (½ stick). Beat mixture until butter is completely incorporated. Add another 4 tablespoons butter, and beat in. Repeat with final 4 tablespoons butter. When completely incorporated, sauce will have thickened sufficiently. Do not overcook. Remove pan from water; let sauce cool slightly. Finely grate enough peeled and seeded cucumber to make ¼ cup; press out all liquid through cheesecloth. Blend grated cucumber into sauce; serve at once.

About 1½ cups.

NOTE: If salted butter is used, omit ¼ teaspoon salt in recipe.

Tartar Sauce

4   scallions, finely chopped
1   small sour pickle, finely chopped
¼   cup pimento-stuffed green olives
1   cup mayonnaise
2   tablespoons parsley, finely chopped
    Salt, white pepper to taste

Combine scallions (white parts only), sour pickle and olives. Blend thoroughly with 1 cup mayonnaise; stir in 2 tablespoons parsley; season to taste with salt and white pepper.

About 1½ cups.

Lobster Sauce

2   cups water
    Shells from lobster tails
2   tablespoons butter
2   tablespoons flour
2   teaspoons hollandaise
2   tablespoons whipped cream
    Salt, pepper to taste

Boil shells in water about 20 minutes, until resulting stock is reduced to approximately 1 cup. Remove shells. Melt butter in a separate saucepan over low heat. Do not brown. Add flour and stir until this roux is well blended. Still stirring roux, add boiling stock all at once and beat strongly to blend in. Turn heat up to moderate, bring sauce to boil, and, while stirring, allow to boil 1 minute. Turn heat to simmer, stir in hollandaise and whipped cream, blend, season with salt and pepper to taste, and remove from heat. Chill and serve.

About 1½ cups.

CHOCOLATE FONDUE

Like all the Swiss fondues, Chocolate Fondue is a guest-participating dish and, as such, is ideal for entertaining. For the hostess who wants to serve something merely sensational but to be away from her guests no more than minutes—whether you call it Fondue Chocolat or plain Chocolate Fondue, serve it to two or 20—it simply deliciously solves that dessert problem.

3 bars Toblerone, 3 ounces each
½ cup cream
2 tablespoons kirsch, Cognac, or Cointreau

Break Toblerone into separate triangular pieces; combine all ingredients in saucepan or small chafing dish. Stir over *low* heat until chocolate is melted and mix is smooth. Serve in chafing dish over low flame.

For dunkables—speared on forks or wooden skewers—serve each person on individual plate one or combination of the following: angel-food cake or ladyfingers, cut into chunks; orange or tangerine slices, strawberries, pineapple chunks (fruit should be well drained); profiteroles of cream-puff pastry, 10 to 12 per person. Dunk, swirl.

Serves 4 to 6.

FONDUE ORIENTALE

½ pound lean beef
½ pound lean veal
½ pound lean pork
   Béarnaise sauce
   Curry sauce
   Tomato sauce
6 tablespoons relish or chopped onion
6 cups chicken stock or bouillon

Slice all meats very thin, in bite-size slices. For easier slicing to thinness required for quick cooking, meats may be partially frozen. Refrigerate meats until 15 minutes before serving.

If homemade sauces are to be served, these may also be prepared well in advance and refrigerated until 15 minutes before serving.

Since this fondue is a cook-it-yourself-at-table dish, set table with fondue pot on burner, in center, where all can reach to dunk-cook. (In lieu of fondue pot, use chafing dish or electric saucepan.) Heat bouillon to boiling (top of stove saves time), transfer to dunking pot, set burner to keep bouillon at low simmering boil.

Serve each diner a plate of meats, about 5 or 6 slices of each of the three listed. On the same plate, or in bowls handy to several diners, serve your variety of sauces. Also give each diner 2 forks, one for spearing and dunk-cooking meat in the pot, the other for dipping cooked meat in sauces and eating. (The cooking fork gets hot.) Each diner cooks meats to doneness he desires. Pork, of course, should be well done. Rice is the perfect side dish for Fondue Orientale, plain or served with butter, in your favorite way, or with a spoonful of the pot bouillon.

When dunking's done, serve the rich broth remaining in the pot in small bowls or in cups for sipping.

Serves 4 to 6.

Tomato Sauce

1	cup tomato ketchup
1	carrot, finely grated
1	clove garlic
1	teaspoon Tabasco
2	teaspoons Worcestershire sauce
2	tablespoons vinegar
2	tablespoons butter

Combine all ingredients. Simmer for 5 minutes.

Mustard Cream Sauce

Stiffly whip ½ cup heavy cream. Fold in 1 tablespoon prepared mustard and season to taste with salt and white pepper.

Lemon-Chili Sauce

Combine ⅔ cup chili sauce with the grated rind of 1 lemon and 1 tablespoon lemon juice.

Makes 1½ cups.

Curry Sauce

3	tablespoons butter
¼	onion, finely chopped
1	green apple, peeled, cored and cubed
2	tablespoons flour
1	tablespoon curry powder
1	cup milk, scalded

The fountain in Central Park, a popular meeting place where one can enjoy a pitcher of sangria under the umbrellas and twin tents of the

Fountain Café.

½ teaspoon salt
2 tablespoons peanut butter

Melt butter. Sauté onions and apple until tender. Sprinkle with a mixture of flour and curry powder. Blend well. Add milk gradually. Add salt and peanut butter. Cook over low heat, stirring constantly, until sauce is smooth and thickened. Serve hot.

Makes about 1½ cups.

Béarnaise Sauce

2 egg yolks
1 tablespoon tarragon vinegar
2 tablespoons cream
¼ teaspoon salt
⅛ teaspoon pepper
4 tablespoons butter
1 teaspoon chopped fresh tarragon
1 teaspoon chopped fresh parsley
1 teaspoon chopped fresh chives

Mix egg yolks, vinegar, cream, salt and pepper in an earthenware bowl. Place bowl over saucepan of hot water over slow fire; stir with whisk until mixture begins to thicken. Add butter, bit by bit, then tarragon, parsley and chives, whisking continuously until thick and well blended.

CHEESE AND ONION PIE

Pastry for 11-inch pie plate
1 tablespoon butter
1 large onion, sliced
½ pound Switzerland Swiss cheese, grated
½ pound Swiss Gruyère, grated

Custard

3 whole eggs
½ cup light cream
½ cup milk
¼ teaspoon salt
¼ teaspoon pepper

Preheat oven to 450° F.

Line pie plate with pastry. Melt butter in a heavy skillet and sauté onion slices until limp.

Sprinkle grated Swiss cheese evenly over pastry. Cover with sautéed onion slices; cover again with grated Gruyère.

Beat eggs lightly and blend with milk, cream, salt and pepper. Pour over cheese onion filling. Bake at 450° F. for 15 minutes, then lower heat to 300° and bake for an additional 30 to 35 minutes. Serve hot.

Serves 6.

VEAL A LA SUISSE

¾   cup butter (clarified)
8   very thin slices of veal
3   tablespoons minced shallots
2   tablespoons flour
½   cup dry white wine
¾   cup heavy cream
¼   teaspoon salt
¼   teaspoon pepper
     Chopped parsley

Melt butter in a heavy saucepan until just liquid and pour off into a sauté pan, leaving sediment to be discarded. Heat clarified butter, add veal slices and sauté until lightly browned. Remove meat to a warm platter, add minced shallots to pan and sauté until limp. Sprinkle with flour and cook 1 minute longer. Add more butter if necessary. Pour in wine and heavy cream, add veal slices and cook over very low heat until sauce thickens. Do not allow to boil. Transfer to a serving dish and garnish with chopped parsley. Serve with hot noodles.

Serves 4.

SWISS CENTER RESTAURANT

4 West 49th Street   *247-6095*

The Swiss Center Restaurant is really three restaurants under one roof, each reflecting a different aspect of Swiss cuisine and a different mood. Most formal of the three is the Swiss Pavilion, an austere, starkly modern, high-ceilinged dining room decorated with the canton flags of Switzerland.

Downstairs the Fondue Pot is a rustic, folksy dining room. Here the tables are bare wood, the timbered ceiling slopes and the decorations are country antiques such as butter molds and old grain sacks.

Most informal of the three is The Bell Bar, where an enormous horseshoe hung with gigantic cowbells dominates the decor. This is the place for a light, quick lunch.

Swiss Center Restaurant is open from noon to 10:00 P.M. On Saturday it is open from 5:00 P.M. to 11:00 P.M. Closed Sunday.

ZUERCHER GESCHNETZELTES
(Sliced Veal in Cream Sauce)

1¼	pounds veal cutlet
	Salt
	Pepper
	Paprika
	Flour
4	tablespoons butter
½	pound mushrooms, sliced
2	shallots, peeled and chopped
½	cup white wine
1	cup canned beef gravy
1	cup heavy cream

Cut veal (or have butcher do it) into thin strips, 2 inches long by ¼ inch wide and ¼ inch thick. Dust the veal slices lightly with salt, pepper, paprika and flour. In a large, heavy skillet melt 3 tablespoons of the butter and quickly sauté the veal till just golden. (If skillet is not large enough, the sautéeing can be done using ½ the butter and veal, and then doing the remainder in a second step.) Remove the veal and set into a colander placed over a bowl to catch the drippings. Add remaining tablespoon of butter to skillet. Add mushrooms and shallots and sauté for about 2 minutes or until golden. Add white wine, bring to a boil and stir for 1 minute. Lower heat, add gravy, meat juices from drained veal and heavy cream.

Keep simmering for about 10 minutes, stirring occasionally, till reduced to about ½ and of a creamy consistency. Adjust seasoning to taste. Add veal to sauce and heat through. Serve with Roesti.

Serves 4–6.

ROESTI
(Traditional Swiss Browned Potatoes)

4   medium potatoes (smooth rather than mealy type)
4   tablespoons butter
    Salt

Boil potatoes in jackets about 45 minutes or until cooked through. Allow to cool. Peel and grate coarsely. Heat butter in 8-inch heavy frying pan. Add potatoes, sprinkle lightly with salt, and stir gently for a few minutes. Stop stirring and allow bottom to become brown and crusty. Turn like a pancake and allow other side to brown. Serve.

WALLISER APRIKOSEN KALTSCHALE
(Cold Apricot Soup)

½   pound dried apricots
1   cup water
¼   cinnamon stick
1   tablespoon lemon juice
1   tablespoon confectioners' sugar
3   7-ounce bottles club soda
2   tablespoons apricot brandy
    Mint leaves

Simmer apricots in water with cinnamon stick for 15 minutes in a covered saucepan. Place in refrigerator till lukewarm. Remove cinnamon stick. Put apricots and juice into blender (most of the water will have been absorbed by the apricots) with 1 bottle of club soda and puree until smooth. Blend in remaining soda. (This will have to be done by halves so blender does not overflow.) Add more soda if a more liquid consistency is desired (and more lemon or sugar according to taste). Add 2 or more tablespoons apricot brandy and refrigerate for several hours or until chilled through. Serve in a bowl set in ice. Garnish with mint leaf if desired.

Serves 8.

SPUMA DI CIOCCOLATE TOBLERONE
(Chocolate Mousse)

1 ½   3-ounce bars Toblerone milk chocolate (triangular bar)
¼   cup water
2   egg whites
2   cups heavy cream

Melt chocolate with water in heavy saucepan over low heat, stirring frequently. Allow to cool to room temperature. Meanwhile, beat egg whites till stiff. In a separate bowl whip cream till light and fluffy. Carefully fold egg whites and whipped cream into chocolate. Pour mixture into individual parfait glasses. Garnish with whipped cream and shredded chocolate. Chill at least 3 hours.

Serves 4–6.

Chapter IV

SCANDINAVIAN FOOD

Restaurants and Recipes

SCANDINAVIA, as anyone will tell you, is where they make that marvelous modern furniture and where there are all those gorgeous blond, blue-eyed girls. Ask them about food and you draw a blank—there's smorgasbord and, of course, Danish pastry and cheese; at least that's the answer if they have never traveled to Denmark, Finland, Norway and Sweden—the four highly diverse countries that make up Scandinavia.

Just as Copenhagen differs from Helsinki and Stockholm bears no resemblance to Oslo, the cuisines of the countries are stamped with their own individuality. Lighthearted Denmark, with its sparkling capital city of Copenhagen, its fields of poppies and daisies, shining clean dairy farms with neat brown cows and pigs so pink they seem to be made of marzipan, has little in common with the mountain-backed fortress city of Oslo, while Stockholm's dignified elegance contrasts sharply with brooding Helsinki, striking in its resemblance to Leningrad.

Denmark's cuisine is a product of its beautiful farms enriched by native seafood. Wonderful cheeses, the very best butter, mild pink hams and rosy-streaked bacon are used lavishly. Pastries glistening yellow with butter are world famous; open-faced sandwiches, *smorrebrod* (*smorre* is the butter, *brod* is the bread), are thickly spread with butter, then laced with ham, mild smoked salmon, herring or cheese. It's simple, straight-forward fare: roast pork with red cabbage, slice of crisp bacon in a parsley sauce, roast capon with frozen cream horseradish. Sweets include unusually good fruit gelatins; red currant and raspberry made from fresh wild fruits and served with lots of *flodeskum* (whipped cream) are favorites. For coffee hours there are finger-shaped macaroons and, of course, pastry.

Denmark makes wonderful beer, and then there's the famous Aallborg Akvavit to drink icy cold in one stinging gulp.

Norway is a country of the sea and it follows that they have perfected simple, uncluttered ways to cook their wonderful shrimp, salmon and cod. Boiled and served with sour-cream sauce or creamed spinach, or better yet smoked and eaten with a horseradish sauce, Norwegian seafood has no equal; fortu-nately for us, it is also shipped all over the world. Norway is also probably the original home of the New England boiled dinner; called "Black Pot," it is a delectable boiled stew of meats and vegetables. Essentially the simplest of Scandinavian cuisine, Norwegian food has an engaging "honest" quality. Perhaps this is best evidenced by the humble cookie; rich with butter and fragrant with caraway seeds, its delicate freshness transforms an everyday food into something special, as indeed it is.

Serenely beautiful Stockholm sets the sophisticated pace for Sweden, and the cuisine is no exception. The capital city of this fantastically prosperous country with its tapestry landscape of flowers and forests, sunlit mountain streams and fairytale castles has a love of gaiety that is reflected in a calendar crowded with festivals, fabulous restaurants and a cuisine that is second to none.

Smorgasbord is as Swedish as Sweden itself, and the large ta-bles laden with a fantastic assortment of delicacies are a delight to anyone who loves good food. In Sweden it is correct to serve yourself three times, first with fish and herring, then cold meats and salads, and finally hot dishes and cheese. Seafood, as in all of Scandinavia, is prepared simply; it's too good to do otherwise, but they do have a knack for a mild cured salmon (*gravlox*) and ship it worldwide, along with their superlative rose pink caviar (*lojrom*).

A sophisticated use of seasoning results in unusually good meat dishes; Swedish meatballs are an international favorite. And there's a wonderful hash called *pytipanna*. Swedish roast goose is so good there's even a festival to celebrate it, St. Martin Gooseday, in late November, somewhat like our Thanksgiving. Food festivals include Crayfish Day on August 8 and an Eel Festival in September, and of course Christmas brings a whole array of festival foods, including the traditional saffron-scented cakes that are served on St. Lucia's Day, December 13, to mark the start of Christmastide.

Coffee and cake are the traditional afternoon snack, as important as the British tea. Sweets for dessert are apt to be in the form of an airy soufflé, unless one elects to serve that most famous of Swedish delicacies, pancakes ablaze with lingonberries and brandy.

Sibelius set the wild, natural magic of Finland to music in his stirring and majestic *Finlandia,* this country of mirror-dark lakes that swallow the light of the low-hanging sky and tall-timbered forest islands. Its capital, Helsinki, bears a strong resemblance to Leningrad, and not too surprisingly the cuisine has more than a touch of Russian influence.

Borsch and blintzes, shashlik and beef stroganoff are commonplace in Helsinki, and vodka, not akvavit, is the preferred drink with the typically Scandinavian dill-flavored crawfish. Strictly Finnish creations include a wonderful oven-roasted stew of lamb, beef and pork called *karjalan paisti; kalakukko,* a meat and herring pie; and the dark pumpernickel bread baked in rings and sold from poles suspended from the bakery ceiling. Typically Finnish, too, are the sweet liqueurs made from native brambleberries and cloudberries. It's an interesting cuisine, perhaps the most unusual in Scandinavia, and proof enough that here are four countries, each sovereign, in the land we call Scandinavia.

The Scandinavians may eat in Manhattan and some of their

75

75

SPECIAL
3 FOR 85¢
HOLLAND HERRING
FOR
PicKling. Chopping
& FRYING

Whole pickled herrings in barrels can be found on the Lower East

Side near the Essex Street Market.

best restaurants are located there, but when they finish the meal they go home to Brooklyn. In 1860, the Swedes and the Norwegians began to arrive in New York in large numbers. The Danish, the smallest of the three Scandinavian groups in the city, reached the height of their migration by 1890. Today New York has about 75,000 Scandinavians. Thirty-seven thousand are Norwegians; 28,000 are Swedish; and the other 10,000 are Danish. And most of them live in Brooklyn.

And while they haven't spawned a plethora of restaurants, together they've managed to give New York some very good examples of smorgasbord, hearty dishes and fish delicacies, all Scandinavian style.

COPENHAGEN
68 West 58th Street   *MU 8-3690*

Koldboard, the Danish version of smorgasbord, is the starring attraction at this cheerfully modern restaurant. A wonderful place to take a family—the almost endless array of delicacies is fascinating to adults and children alike. And don't be surprised to see some of the country's most famous Scandinavians dining here.

Copenhagen serves lunch from noon to 3:00 P.M. and dinner from 5:30 P.M. to 11:00 P.M. Closed Sunday.

FISH SOUFFLÉ
    ¼   cup fine dry bread crumbs
    1¾   pounds white fish, haddock or cod
    1   teaspoon salt
    1½   tablespoons cornstarch
    1¼   cups light cream
    ¾   cup heavy cream

Butter a 1½-quart mold or casserole and sprinkle evenly with fine dry bread crumbs. Cut fish into small pieces and sprinkle with salt. Cream cornstarch with a little of the light cream until absolutely smooth. Combine with the rest of light and heavy cream and mix well. Place ¼ of the fish in the electric blender, blend a moment on high speed to break up fish, add ¼ of the cream-cornstarch mixture, blend at high speed until very fluffy, transfer fish-cream mixture to a mixing bowl and repeat the process, using only ¼ of the fish and cream at a time, until all ingredients are blended. *Do not attempt to blend all of the fish and cream at once.* Whip the mixture with a slotted spoon until very light, pour into prepared mold, cover tightly with buttered aluminum foil, and tie on securely with string. Place mold in a shallow pan of hot water and bake in a moderate oven (350° F.) for about 50 minutes or until a silver knife inserted in the center comes out clean. Serve with melted butter and boiled new potatoes.

Serves 6.

SCANDIA

227 West 45th Street CI 6-6600

True Swedish smorgasbord; there's even a little card that explains how best to enjoy it in true Swedish style.

The Scandia smorgasbord, as well as regular dishes, is available from noon to 3:00 P.M., from 4:30 P.M. to 1:00 A.M. On Sunday the restaurant is open from noon to 10:30 P.M.

ROAST PORK WITH PRUNES

14	large prunes
2	to 2½ pounds pork tenderloin
1	teaspoon salt
½	teaspoon freshly ground black pepper
3	tablespoons akvavit
3	tablespoons butter
½	cup fresh orange juice
½	cup dry white wine

Soak prunes in hot water until plumped. Drain and remove pits by slitting with a sharp knife.

Trim excess fat off tenderloin; with a sharp knife cut tenderloin lengthwise about ⅔ through. Arrange prunes in a neat

The famous sculpture of "Standing Woman" by Lachaise in the garden of the Museum of Modern Art, overlooking the museum's

outdoor restaurant.

row inside tenderloin. Fasten together by tying tightly with butcher's string. Rub with salt and pepper.

Heat butter in heavy flameproof casserole or sauté pan, one with a cover. Brown the tenderloin evenly in the hot butter. When it is thoroughly browned, pour off any remaining fat and add the akvavit. Heat briefly, then flame by touching a lighted match to the hot liquid. When the flame dies out, add orange juice and wine. Cover tightly and bake in a slow oven 250° to 300° F. for 1½ to 2 hours. Slice and serve hot or cold.

Serves 4.

DRIED FRUIT SOUP

½	cup dried apples
½	cup dried prunes
½	cup dried peaches
½	cup dried apricots
7	cups water
2	cups sugar
1	stick cinnamon
1	lemon cut into thin slices
¼	cup tapioca

Soak the fruits in the water overnight in a large, heavy enamelized saucepan. Add sugar, and in the same water in which it was soaked cook fruit over low heat for 20 to 25 minutes or until very tender. Strain through a sieve, pressing fruit with the back of a spoon to extract juice. Return juice to saucepan, add cinnamon stick, stir in tapioca, add lemon slices. Cook briefly until clear and slightly thickened. Remove cinnamon stick. Serve hot or cold.

Serves 4.

GRAVLOX

(Swedish Marinated Salmon)

7	to 8 pounds middle-cut fresh salmon, in 1 piece
½	cup salt
½	cup sugar
1	tablespoon whole white pepper, crushed

1   tablespoon whole allspice, crushed
2   large bunches fresh dill
8   tablespoons Cognac
     Lemon wedges
     Black pepper
     Mustard sauce (see below)

Clean salmon, leave skin on, slit carefully with a sharp knife and remove bone, being careful not to break fish. You should have two large fillets. Rinse in ice water and pat dry. Mix salt, sugar, pepper and allspice and rub well into all sides of the fillets. Wash dill and place ⅓ of it in a large nonmetal bowl or pan. Sprinkle fillets with 4 tablespoons of the Cognac and place 1 fillet skin side down on top of the dill, cover with another ⅓ of the dill, sprinkle with Cognac, top with second fillet, skin side up, and spread remaining Cognac. Place a weighted plate or board on top of the fish and refrigerate for 36 hours. Drain well, scrape off dill and cut in thin slices at a slant away from the skin. Serve cold with lemon wedges and freshly ground black pepper.

About 20 servings as an appetizer or part of a smorgasbord buffet supper.

Mustard Sauce

2   tablespoons dry mustard
½   cup cream
1   tablespoon finely chopped fresh dill
1   teaspoon sugar
     Pinch of salt

Blend mustard with 2 tablespoons of the cream to make a smooth paste; add remaining cream, dill, sugar and salt, and blend well.

SWEDISH BEEF LINDSTROM

4   small potatoes
1   tablespoon butter (room temperature)
¼   cup cream
2   pounds ground tenderloin
2   egg yolks

1½   teaspoons salt
1   teaspoon freshly ground black pepper
½   cup finely chopped cooked beets
½   cup finely chopped onion
½   cup finely chopped capers
        Butter for frying

Boil potatoes until tender, peel and put through ricer or food mill while still hot, add butter and cream, and beat until light and fluffy. Add meat, egg yolks, salt and pepper, and blend well. Combine beets, onions and capers, and add to meat mixture. Mix lightly with a fork until well blended. Form mixture into large, flat cakes. Heat butter in heavy sauté pan and brown cakes quickly on both sides. Serve at once.

Makes 10 to 12 large cakes.

FRASARE MED SKANSK POTATIS
(Beef with Potatoes)

12   small boiled new potatoes
6   small fillets of beef or tournedos
           (not too thick, about ¼ inch)
2   tablespoons butter
½   cup cream
1   teaspoon butter
1   tablespoon flour
1   teaspoon paprika

Peel potatoes and cut into small dice. Sprinkle evenly over the bottom of shallow casserole. Allow tournedos or fillets to come to room temperature. Melt the 2 tablespoons butter in a heavy sauté pan and brown fillets about 3 minutes on each side for medium well done. Place on top of potatoes in casserole. Pour excess fat from sauté pan, add cream and cook over low heat for 1 or 2 minutes. Blend the 1 teaspoon of butter with flour to make a smooth ball and add to hot cream, blend well and cook only until sauce is slightly thickened. Stir in paprika and pour over meat and potato casserole. Bake in a 400° F. oven for 5 to 10 minutes until heated through. Serve at once.

Serves 6.

STOCKHOLM RESTAURANT

151 West 51st Street   *CI 6-6560*

When Stockholm Restaurant first opened in the 1930s, its diners were chiefly Scandinavians who missed the variety-laden smorgasbord of their homeland. Like all good things, the smorgasbord idea spread quickly, and now the Stockholm's clientele is as varied as its table.

Stockholm Restaurant is open every day from noon to 1:00 A.M.

SWEDISH CHRISTMAS GLOGG

2	whole cardamom seeds
4	whole cloves
1	cinnamon stick
2	peppercorns
2	cups water
½	cup white raisins
½	cup blanched almonds
1	bottle Burgundy wine
1	bottle port wine
1	strip orange rind (yellow part only)
	Akvavit
	Light rum
	Cognac
	Sugar to taste

Place cardamom seeds, cloves, cinnamon stick and peppercorns in a small cheesecloth bag. Tie securely and place in saucepan with water. Bring to a quick boil, then lower heat and let simmer until water has reduced to about half. Add raisins, almonds, wine and orange rind, bring quickly to boil, then remove from heat. Remove and discard orange rind. Refrigerate covered for 12 hours or longer. Remove cheesecloth bag of spices.

To serve, reheat and pour into thick mugs. Add about 1 teaspoon akvavit, rum and Cognac to each mug. Stir in a few raisins and almonds. Add sugar to taste and serve at once.

Serves 12 or more.

Both buyer and seller of hot pretzels seem very satisfied with the transaction in front of Bergdorf Goodman's elegant and fashionable store on Fifth Avenue.

HERRING SALAD

1   salt herring
      Water
      Milk
1   cup diced cooked beets
1   apple, cored and diced, not peeled
2   ribs celery, diced
2   teaspoons capers, drained
2   hard-cooked eggs, chopped
      Pepper
⅓   cup heavy cream
½   teaspoon prepared mustard
1   tablespoon white vinegar
¼   teaspoon salt
½   teaspoon sugar
      Lettuce leaves
      Chopped parsley

Wash herring under cold running water. Place in nonmetal bowl and cover with half water, half milk. Cover and marinate in refrigerator 6 to 8 hours. Drain and pat dry with paper toweling. Cut off and discard tail and head. Remove all bones and cut into small pieces.

Combine in mixing bowl herring, beets, apple, celery, capers and hard-cooked eggs. Season with pepper and mix lightly.

Mix cream with vinegar and mustard. Season with salt and sugar. Add to herring mixture and blend well. Serve on lettuce leaves. Garnish with parsley.

Serves 4 to 5.

KORT LAMM MED DILLSAS
(Lamb with Dill)

3   pounds shoulder of lamb, trimmed of excess fat
      Boiling water
2   teaspoons salt
5   peppercorns
5   sprigs fresh dill
1   bay leaf
      Dill sauce (see below)
      Boiled potatoes

Place lamb in large saucepan. Add boiling water to cover. Let boil for 5 minutes. Remove from heat and drain.

Cover again with boiling water. Bring to a full boil and skim surface until clear. Add salt, peppercorns, dill and bay leaf. Reduce heat, cover and let simmer for 2 hours or until meat is tender.

Remove meat from stock. Place in covered dish. Refrigerate until ready to reheat.

Strain stock and refrigerate until fat has congealed and risen to surface. Remove and discard fat.

About 30 minutes before serving reheat meat in strained stock. Remove meat from stock (reserve stock for sauce), cut into serving pieces and place on heated platter. Keep warm while preparing sauce.

Serves 8.

Dill Sauce

3	tablespoons butter
2	tablespoons flour
1½	cups reserved stock
2	tablespoons white wine vinegar
1	teaspoon sugar
	Salt to taste
2	egg yolks, lightly beaten
¼	cup chopped fresh dill

Melt the butter over low heat. Add the flour and stir until well blended. Slowly add stock, stirring constantly as it is added. Cook, stirring almost constantly, until sauce begins to thicken. Add vinegar and sugar. Season with salt to taste. Remove from heat and quickly stir in egg yolks. Return to heat, add dill and cook over low heat, stirring, until sauce is quite thick and smooth. Do not allow to boil.

Pour some of the sauce over the sliced meat. Pass remaining sauce at the table. Serve with boiled potatoes.

Serves 8.

SWEDISH MEATBALLS

2	tablespoons butter
½	cup finely chopped onion

½	cup fresh bread crumbs
½	cup light cream
½	pound ground beef tenderloin
½	pound ground veal
¼	pound ground pork
2	teaspoons salt
1	teaspoon freshly ground black pepper
⅛	teaspoon ground cloves
¼	cup butter
¼	cup dry white wine

Heat butter in heavy sauté pan and cook onions in it until soft but not brown. Combine onions, bread crumbs, cream, beef, veal, pork and spices. Blend well but lightly with a fork. Shape into small balls. Handle as little as possible to keep light. Heat butter in heavy, deep sauté pan and fry meatballs until brown on all sides, turning constantly to prevent sticking. When meat is brown, pour off excess fat, add wine and barely simmer over very low heat for 5 or 6 minutes. Serve on cocktail picks for smorgasbord.

Serves 6 to 8 as part of a smorgasbord buffet supper.

A view across Third Avenue of P. J. Clarke's, the most famous pub of them all in New York, where you might see anybody, from Jackie and Ari Onassis to Liz Taylor and Richard Burton, at one time or another. The menu is written on a blackboard in the back room.

Chapter V

SPANISH FOOD

~~~~~~

Restaurants and Recipes

SPAIN is a world apart, separated by mountains from Europe, by water from Africa and separated even from other Spanish-speaking people by culture and cuisine.

In New York there are 25,000 Spaniards, and they come from nearly every region of Spain, among them Madrid, Barcelona and Catalonia, Galicia and the Basque provinces.

The largest Spanish settlement is in the area of West 14th Street. This is also where many of the Spanish food stores are found. But Spaniards live everywhere in the city, and in fact the Spanish Pavilion, one of the city's finest restaurants and the only one that features the *alta cocina (haute cuisine)* of Spain, is located in the most fashionable section of Park Avenue.

SPANISH FOOD

Of all the cuisines of Europe the Spanish has a simplicity and an engaging "honest" quality that stem from an almost fanatical regard for fresh ingredients. Too often Spanish food is described as "spicy" or "hot" when just the opposite is true; Spaniards

A scene from Rincon de Espagne, an authentic Spanish restaurant on Thompson Street in Greenwich Village.

rarely use spices, and heavily spiced foods of other countries are anathema to Spanish palates.

Seafood in all its infinite variety, lobsters, prawns, trout and salmon, abound and they are prepared in the simplest of ways. Even a seemingly intricate dish such as Zarzula de Mariscos Costa Brava is really only a simple fish stew, the only seasoning, salt, tarragon and sherry. Meats are grilled or roasted, soups are plain and substantial, and dessert is more often than not a caramel custard, flan or fresh fruits.

But for all its simplicity Spanish food is infinitely good; from the early-morning chocolate and crusty roll or hot, crisp pastry, to the five-course 2:00 P.M. *comida* and a 6:00 snack of pastries and coffee, the *merienda,* tapis and sherry at 8:00, to dinner around 10:00 P.M., the Spaniard dines on a cuisine as interesting and varied as any on earth.

It is not at all unusual for a Castilian to begin the *comida* with a salad of artichokes, peas, asparagus, beans, onions, slices of sausage and olives; proceed to hot garlic soup with a poached egg, followed by fresh grilled fish, roast capons or meat, cheese, flan and/or fruit, perhaps strawberries in Valencia orange juice. The point is fresh food, simply cooked, all with an artist's regard for composing a memorable meal.

As in all great cuisine the secret of success is in the integrity of the cook—and that is exportable, happily for New Yorkers, who can bask literally in the "flavor of Spain."

THE SPANISH PAVILION

475 Park Avenue   *421-5690*

One of the most elegant restaurants in New York, with prices to match. Admittedly expensive, it is nonetheless worth the price, for here at last is *alta cocina Español,* the *haute cuisine* of Spain.

Against a background of sixteenth-century tapestries and original Goya drawings, the exquisite food is served by a legion of swift-handed Spanish waiters, personally trained by owner Alberto Heras, a perfectionist to match Henri Soule himself.

A little bit of old Spain on MacDougal Street in Greenwich Village.

The Spanish Pavilion serves lunch from noon to 3:00 P.M. and dinner from 5:30 P.M. to 1:00 A.M. No lunch is served on Saturday. Closed Sunday.

SOPA CASTILLA LA VIEJA

(Almond Soup)

1	long loaf French bread
1/3	cup Spanish olive oil
1/2	cup chopped blanched almonds
2 1/2	cups chicken consommé
2 1/2	cups beef consommé
	Salt to taste
	Slivered almonds

Cut French bread into thin slices, toast and set aside.

Heat oil in a small saucepan, add almonds and sauté until golden. Transfer to electric blender and blend until pureed.

Combine and heat chicken and beef consommés and add salt to taste. Pour into individual ovenproof earthenware bowls. Spread almond puree on toast and float on top of soup. Place under broiler heat until almonds are toasted. Sprinkle each serving with slivered almonds and serve.

Makes 4 servings.

COMPOTA DE FRUTA AL VINO DE RIOJA

(Stewed Fruit in Rioja Wine)

3 1/2	cups Spanish red Rioja wine
1 1/4	cups water
1	cinnamon stick
1	cup sugar
1	pound apples, peeled, seeded and sliced
1	pound pears, peeled, seeded and cubed
1/2	pound mixed dried fruits—peaches, prunes, figs and raisins

Mix wine with water; add cinnamon and sugar. Place over medium heat and cook, stirring occasionally, until sugar has dissolved. Add fruit and bring to boil, then lower heat and let simmer until fruit is tender, about 15 to 20 minutes. Serve hot or cold.

Makes 6 servings.

ZARZUELA DE MARISCOS COSTA BRAVA

1	1½-pound live lobster
12	clams
12	mussels
12	red Spanish shrimp
12	jumbo shrimp
½	pound boneless red snapper or sea bass
6	tablespoons butter
⅓	cup Spanish brandy
½	cup Spanish dry sherry
¼	cup heavy cream
	Fish sauce (see below)
½	cup fresh bread crumbs
1	tablespoon chopped parsley
¼	teaspoon tarragon
	Salt to taste
6	slices of fried bread (see below)

Have your fish market prepare and clean lobster; cut off head (use in sauce below), remove large claws, crack shells and remove meat. Remove tail and cut crosswise into 4 pieces, leaving shell on.

Clean clams and mussels thoroughly. Place mussels in a large pot with about ½ cup water; cover and place over medium heat and let steam until shells open, about 20 minutes.

Cut snapper or bass into 1-inch chunks. Sprinkle lightly with salt.

Heat butter in a large, shallow paella pan until bubbly but not browned. Add all seafood and fish; cook over high heat for about 5 minutes. Reduce heat to moderate.

Pour in warmed brandy and ignite. Add sherry and let flame subside; stir in cream and cook, stirring, until sauce is reduced by about half. Add fish sauce; sprinkle with bread crumbs, parsley and tarragon. Cook, stirring often, for a final 6 to 8 minutes.

Serve in shallow soup plates garnished with triangles of fried bread.

Serves 4.

Fish Sauce

⅓   cup olive oil
    Head from lobster (see instructions for preparing fish)
1   carrot, scraped and diced
1   leek, chopped
2   ribs celery, chopped
1   small white onion, peeled and chopped
1   clove garlic, peeled and minced
2   medium tomatoes or 1 large one, chopped
1   cup dry white wine
1   cup fish stock (substitute clam juice if desired)
1   cup beef stock
⅓   cup raw rice
1   tablespoon paprika
½   cup ground blanched almonds
    Salt and pepper to taste

Break up lobster head in a mortar.

Heat oil in a large heavy saucepan. Add lobster head, carrot, leek, onion, and garlic. Sauté until onion is limp, about five minutes. Stir in remaining ingredients except ground almonds. Cover and let simmer over low heat for 2 hours. Strain through sieve lined with double-thick cheesecloth. Transfer to a second saucepan and stir in ground almonds. Set aside.

Fried Bread

¼   cup olive oil
6   slices firm day-old white bread, crust removed

Heat oil in a shallow skillet. Cut bread slices in half horizontally to make triangles. Fry in hot oil until golden brown on both sides. Drain on paper towels.

JAI ALAI
82 Bank Street   *989-5826*

Jai Alai has a persistent if quiet quality that has seen it through 50 years at the same location. Opened originally for Spanish and Basque people in New York, the word spread quickly that this was the place for good Northern Spanish food. The setting is Iberian-inspired.

Jai Alai is open from 11:00 A.M to midnight. On Sunday it opens at 1:00 P.M.

EGGS MALAGUEÑA

2	tablespoons vegetable oil
1	large onion, peeled and chopped
1	small green pepper, seeded and chopped
½	clove garlic, minced
2	cups (canned) Italian plum tomatoes and juice
1	tablespoon tomato paste
2	(canned) *serrano* chilies, drained, rinsed in cold water and chopped
1	teaspoon sugar
1	teaspoon salt
2	*chorizo* (Spanish pork sausage)
1	teaspoon lard
1	cup cooked green peas
1	(canned) pimento, cut into narrow strips
6	eggs

Heat the oil in a large saucepan. Add onion, green pepper and garlic. Sauté until vegetables are soft, but not browned. Add tomatoes, tomato paste, chilies, sugar and salt. Cook, stirring occasionally, over low heat for 25 to 30 minutes.

Cut *chorizo* into bite-size slices. Heat lard and cook slices until lightly browned. Drain and add to sauce.

Spoon sauce into 6 individual shallow ovenproof casseroles. Spoon peas and pimentos around outer edge. Add 1 or 2 slices

Entrance to the great Spanish market near Harlem, uptown East

Side Manhattan.

of sausage, then break egg into center. Cover and bake in pre-heated 375° F. oven until eggs have set, about 5 minutes.

Serves 6.

FORNOS

236 West 52nd Street   *CI 7-9420*

Fornos has been turning out good Spanish food for nearly 50 years, and its Spanish clientele is grateful. It is close to Broadway's theatres and a congenial place to eat before or after the show.

Fornos is open from noon to midnight. On Saturday the hours are 4:00 P.M. to midnight. Closed Sunday.

PAELLA

1½	dozen clams (in their shells)
	Salt
1	1½- to 2½-pound chicken, cut up for sauté
4	tablespoons flour
4	tablespoons oil
1	cup raw rice
½	teaspoon saffron
½	teaspoon salt
¼	teaspoon pepper
2	cups chicken stock
2	cups water
3	tablespoons bacon drippings
1	large green pepper, seeded and diced
4	medium onions, peeled and chopped
1	clove garlic, peeled and minced
1	package frozen peas
2	pounds shrimp, shelled and deveined

Soak clams in cold salted water for one hour. Scrub shells with a stiff brush. Refrigerate until ready to use. Wash and dry chicken pieces well. Dredge evenly with flour. Heat oil in a deep heavy pan and cook chicken over medium heat until well browned. Turn heat to low, add rice, saffron, salt and pepper;

cook, stirring, for one or two minutes until rice is coated with oil. Add chicken stock and water. Simmer over low heat until rice is almost tender and almost all liquid has been absorbed. Remove from heat. Heat bacon drippings in a separate fry pan and sauté green pepper, onions and garlic until tender and lightly browned. Add to rice and chicken mixture. Add frozen peas, clams and shrimp. Transfer to a large casserole. Add a little more chicken stock if the mixture seems dry.

Cover and bake in a preheated 350° F. oven for 20 to 25 minutes or until clams have opened and paella is very hot.

Serves 6–8.

In the Spanish market uptown one can buy all the exotic foods of the tropics. Note the sign on the wall behind the stand saying, "Make Love."

PART II

English and Irish Food

Chapter VI

ENGLISH FOOD

~~~~~~

Restaurants and Recipes

In the past 30 years at least 175,000 people have come to New York from Great Britain. In 1962 and 1963 alone, no other country except Italy sent more people. And a far larger number of New Yorkers are descended from the British who had been the city's Colonial settlers.

For the most part, there is no geographically distinct English community in New York, and because the English speak the same language—or at least a similar one—as the Americans, they are very easily assimilated. After a generation, or less, their English ancestry is barely apparent.

But there is one aspect of English life that has always existed in New York and has recently been stronger than ever. That is the flood of English restaurants and pubs. They all, of course, feature the standard cuisine of the English. But more than that, they serve it in a setting right out of old England, and they manage to capture the spirit and feeling of the best of the British Isles.

The colorful little mews houses of MacDougal Alley, Greenwich Village.

THE FOODS OF ENGLAND

As Lord Emsworth put it, there's nothing like good plain British cooking, and this befuddled hero of P. G. Wodehouse's tales of Blandings Castle was right. In fact, the perfect way to wind up a tour of Europe or a tour of European restaurants is with good, plain English food. After *aroz con pollo, blanquette de veau, sauerbraten,* and *pasta à la romana* plus a sprinkling of smorgasbord, nothing has quite so much appeal as an excellent cut of plain roast beef with roast potatoes.

The best of English cooking is stately home cooking, rack of lamb with mint sauce, steak and kidney pudding, Dover sole, and of course first, last and always superb roast beef with Yorkshire pudding. For dessert there's always trifle, that cozy combination of sponge cake, jam and custard with a little wine to give it daring, and the lovely, comforting puddings: Lord Emsworth's favorite—roly poly with lots of jam, or for festive occasions plum, ablaze with brandy.

From the traditional English breakfast with its kippers, ham, eggs, muffins and marmalade through lunch, afternoon tea and dinner the solid feeling of well-being pervades. All sorts of little extras are provided. When one lunches in a pub, there's an endless array of cheeses, hams, potted shrimps, cold meat puddings. Tea is never just tea; little sandwiches, sweet buns and cake are the bare minimum. And at dinner there's a "savory" of cheese, meat or fish (after the usual four courses) followed by a tray of little cakes and glazed fruit. Then, port or brandy with an accompanying bowl of walnuts.

England is a man's country, but the ladies seem to fare pretty well. Generally there's a no-nonsense attitude about cooking that makes for good daily fare. Like all cuisines, English food reflects the climate and the temper of the people. England's cool summers and cold, damp winters make substantial fare more appealing. Nothing is so completely satisfying as to come in out of a cold rain to find a laden tea table in front of an open fire.

Country people at heart despite sprawling London and the grimy mill towns, the English have brought country living to a fine art, and with it a love of hunting that goes back deep into

Chess buffs test their skill endlessly at Washington Square Park,

Greenwich Village.

the English history. The beloved roast meat and game pies are part of the heritage. Part, too, a love of picnicking, brought about probably by the need for a portable lunch for the hunt, but developed into a feast by the Edwardians with their hampers of cold game and chilled champagne. To this day the English make the most marvelous picnic baskets in the world. In fact, if you want to see picnicking brought to its height, go to one of the superb performances at Glyndebourne deep in Sussex for an unforgettable sight of men and women in full evening regalia having a picnic supper on the green lawns around the opera house.

There's a no-nonsense, cozy attitude about drinking, too. In fact, the English pub is about the most comforting place on earth, and what could be more sensible than good dry gin or an honest whiskey? Not for the English the syrupy liqueurs, the complicated cocktail or the fruit-decorated sour or collins. A splash of tonic in the gin, of water in the whiskey; anything else wouldn't make good English sense. Beer and stout are second favorites as far as alcohol is concerned, but the national beverages are gin, whiskey, and the immortal British cup of tea.

CHESHIRE CHEESE RESTAURANT

319 West 51st Street   *765-0616*

The name, the owners, the menu, the food and the beer are thoroughly British here. And so is the atmosphere, helped by the dark beams, horse brasses, pewter tankards, wrought-iron wall lamps, red tablecloths and soft lighting. Cheshire Cheese Restaurant is all you've ever dreamed an English pub to be—unless you've been to England and know this dream of a place is even better than the original.

Cheshire Cheese serves lunch from noon to 3:00 P.M. and dinner from 5:30 P.M. to 9:00 P.M. No lunch is served on Saturday. Closed Sunday and Monday.

BAKEWELL TART

Pastry for 8-inch pie plate
4 tablespoons raspberry jam
1 cup ground almonds (previously blanched)
¾ cup extra-fine granulated sugar
2 eggs
2 tablespoons sweet butter (melted)
¼ teaspoon almond extract
¼ cup heavy cream

Preheat oven to 400° F.

Line pie plate (ovenproof) with pastry. Flute edge, spread with jam. Mix almonds and sugar; beat eggs lightly and add to almond-sugar mixture. Add melted butter and almond extract. Mix well. Pour into pie plate and bake at 400° F. for 15 minutes. Lower heat to 300° F. and continue to bake for an additional 30 minutes. Chill well. Whip cream and garnish tart just before serving.

Serves 6.

SHERRY TRIFLE

24 ladyfingers
½ cup cream sherry
¼ cup strawberry jam
2 cups boiled custard, cooled (see below)
½ cup heavy cream

Line bottom of a glass serving dish with ladyfingers, add sherry, spread with strawberry jam. Cover with boiled custard. Chill well. Just before serving whip cream and pile lightly over surface of trifle.

Serves 6.

Boiled Custard

1¾ cups milk, scalded
5 egg yolks
¼ cup sugar
Sherry to taste

Place milk in saucepan and heat almost to boiling. Remove from heat at once. Meanwhile, beat egg yolks until light and fluffy, add sugar and sherry, and pour in scalded milk. Blend well. Cook in top half of a double boiler over barely simmering water until custard has thickened. Stir constantly. Cool before using for trifle.

ENGLISH-STYLE PRIME RIBS OF BEEF

1   8- to 10-pound prime rib roast
    Salt

NOTE: Small roasts do not cook properly, according to the Cheshire Cheese chef. Select an 8- or 10-pound (or even larger) roast for best results.

Preheat oven to 400° F., rub roast with salt, place fat side up in roasting pan and cook uncovered for 20 minutes to the pound for rare roast, 25 to 30 minutes for each pound for medium well.

When roast reaches the desired degree of doneness, remove from oven and let stand in a cool place for 3 to 4 hours. Skim fat from pan and reheat roast quickly (about 20 minutes), basting with juices that have accumulated in the pan. Transfer to serving platter and carve in paper-thin slices. Serve natural gravy separately.

Serves 12 to 16.

STEAK AND KIDNEY PIE

Pastry

1¾   cups flour
⅛   teaspoon salt
¾   cup butter
½   cup ice water
1   teaspoon lemon juice

Sift flour and salt together; blend in butter with pastry blender or fork. Mix ice water with lemon juice and add enough to flour-butter mixture to make a soft dough. Roll into a ball, cover with wax paper and chill for at least one hour.

Filling

1¾ pounds stewing beef, cut into squares
¼ cup flour
½ teaspoon pepper
⅛ pound salt pork, cut into cubes
1 small onion, peeled and chopped
1½ cups beef stock
6 lamb kidneys, split
1 tablespoon minced parsley

Preheat oven to 450° F. Roll beef in flour seasoned with pepper. Place salt pork in heavy sauté pan and cook over medium heat until enough fat accumulates to sauté onion until limp but not brown. Place onion in large, deep casserole. Sauté floured beef until nicely browned on all sides. Add to casserole with remaining crisp cubes of salt pork. Coat the lamb kidneys with remaining flour and add all to casserole. Pour beef stock over meat and onions; sprinkle with parsley. Roll out pastry to ⅛-inch thickness, cover dish with crust and seal with a narrow strip of pastry moistened with milk and fluted to edge of casserole with a fork. Cut slits for steam.

Bake at 450° F. for 20 minutes or until crust is lightly browned. Reduce heat to 300° F. and continue to cook for 1 to 1½ hours. If crust becomes too brown, cover with a sheet of aluminum foil. Serve hot or (English style) cold with beer.

Serves 6.

YORKSHIRE PUDDING

1 cup flour
⅛ teaspoon salt
1 egg
1 cup milk
    Beef drippings from roast

Preheat oven to 350° F.

Mix flour and salt in a large bowl. Make a "well" in the center and break egg into it. Add milk a small amount at a time, beating with a wire whisk as it is added. Beat until smooth. Grease a square baking pan with beef drippings and heat pan in the oven for 5 to 10 minutes. Pour pudding into pan and bake until it has risen and is well browned, about 20 to 25 minutes. Actually the original English way was to pour the pudding into the still hot roasting pan when the roast was removed, allowing the accumulated roast drippings to add flavor to the pudding—probably easier and better. Either way, it's a necessity with prime ribs of beef.

Serves 6.

Chapter VII

IRISH FOOD

~~~~~~

Restaurants and Recipes

COME ST. PATRICK'S DAY in New York City, with the firemen, the policemen, the bands, schoolchildren and just about everyone else marching, you might think the whole town came from the ould sod. But if you waited until the next day to count, you'd find there's really about a half million Irish in New York.

One of the first of the great waves of immigrants to the United States, the Irish fled, sick and feeble, from the great famine of the 1840s. So many came to New York that at one time the Irish accounted for one-fourth of the population of the city.

Today, although the Irish are now scattered throughout the city, parts of Third Avenue and of the West Side still have a Hibernian flavor. And this flavor is most easily found in the proliferation of pubs and restaurants with the atmosphere of Erin. Most are handsome, many serve decent to delicious food, all are friendly and cozy and nice to visit, even when it's not St. Patrick's Day.

IRISH FOOD

Irish food is as hard to pin down as the Irish. It can be as sophisticated as the famed Galway oysters and Dublin prawns

151

New Yorkers on a hot summer day taking a ride on the Staten Island ferry, which still costs only a nickel each way. The Statue of Liberty can be seen at left.

prepared in the grill room of Dublin's luxe Russell Hotel, or as simple and earthy as the wonderful soda bread and inevitable Irish stew. Whichever it is, the Irish have a talent for enjoying life and make provision for it with their convivial pubs, spirited hunts, elegant formal dinner parties and cozy afternoon teas. And who but the Irish would have had the inspired idea of adding whiskey to blazing hot coffee, a drink that has probably brought more pleasure to more people than there are gallons of water in the River Liffey?

Beginning with a breakfast of oatmeal, Irish bacon, deep brown bread, marmalade and tea, through dinner of salmon, beef, potatoes and pudding, Irish food is substantial and satisfying. It's a satisfying country with its gentle, dreamy haze and its emerald-green parks and fields. Moreover, the Irish themselves, considerate and friendly (as long as one is not a bore!), make it one of the pleasantest of all countries for a holiday.

This same genuine concern and innate hospitality flow like Guinness stout in New York's Irish pubs and restaurants. Probably nowhere else will you find the warmth of welcome so evident. Lunch or dine in an Irish pub when you are not in a hurry; there should always be time for another glass, another story to hear, another to tell.

JOHN BARLEYCORN

209 East 45th Street   *YU 6-1088*

What a handsome Irish pub this is, with its pewter serving plates, old etchings, stained glass, brick walls, covered lanterns and lilting brogues.

Lunch is served from noon to 3:00 P.M. and dinner from 5:00 P.M. to 1:30 A.M. No lunch is served on weekends.

KILLARNEY BEEF STEW

¼ pound salt pork, cut into cubes
2 pounds beef stew meat, cut into cubes
6 small onions, peeled and chopped

6	medium potatoes, peeled and quartered
6	carrots, scraped and cut in half
1	quart beef stock
½	teaspoon pepper
2	tablespoons flour
3	tablespoons parsley
¼	cup Irish whiskey

Fry salt pork in deep, heavy sauté pan (2-quart size) until golden brown, remove and reserve for garnish. Brown the meat over medium-high heat, add the onions and cook until transparent. Add potatoes and carrots and cook briefly, stirring constantly, until lightly browned and glazed. Add stock and pepper and cook over low heat until meat and vegetables are tender.

Remove meat and vegetables to serving bowl and keep warm. Reduce stock by boiling rapidly for 10 to 15 minutes. Make a paste of the flour and a little of the hot stock, and add to pan. Stir over medium heat for 5 or 6 minutes to blend and thicken. Add Irish whiskey and cook 1 minute longer. Pour over meat and vegetables; garnish with parsley and salt pork cubes.

Serves 6.

CHARLEY O'S BAR & GRILL & BAR

33 West 48th Street   *582-7141*

Oh, the joy of Charley O's. It may not be a perfect Dublin copy, but it is surely the world's most elegant saloon. And a friendlier place you're not likely to find.

The restaurant is on the large size and so are the two bars— one for that marvelous foaming draught beer, the other for thick sandwiches, oysters and clams.

Charley O's is open for lunch from 11:45 A.M. to 3:00 P.M. and for dinner from 5:00 P.M. to 10:00 P.M. Supper is served from 10:00 P.M. to 12:30 A.M. On Sunday brunch is served from noon to 3:30 P.M.

Ros Cole with John Cohane at Biddy Mulligan's.

SOUSED SHRIMP

  2 carrots, scraped and sliced
  1 onion, peeled and quartered
  2 lemons cut in half
  2 ribs celery, chopped
  5 bay leaves
  ½ teaspoon salt
  5 pounds raw shrimp

In a saucepan of cold water, add carrots, onion, lemon halves, celery, bay leaves and salt. Bring the water to a boil and add the shrimp. As soon as the water comes to a boil again, shrimp are cooked.

Immediately drain off the water from the saucepan and allow the pan to stand under cold running water until the shrimp are cooled (at least 10 minutes). Remove shrimp and peel off shells. Be sure to devein the shrimp. (The vein is the black thin stripe running from the head to the tail of the shrimp.) The shrimp are now ready for marination.

Makes 12 portions.

Marinade

   2 pounds onions, finely sliced
   8 lemons, finely sliced
  12 bay leaves
   1 bunch fresh tarragon, finely chopped
   2 cups olive oil
   2 tablespoons tarragon vinegar
     Dash of Worcestershire sauce
     Dash of Tabasco sauce
     Salt and pepper to taste

Combine all the ingredients in a large bowl. This should take at least 10 minutes to ensure that all the ingredients are *thoroughly* mixed together.

Now add the cooked shrimp, a few at a time, to the marinade. Continue to stir the marinade until all the shrimp are in the bowl. Allow to stand in the refrigerator for a minimum of 12 hours. Serve cold.

CHARLEY O'S IRISH LAMB STEW

     2   pounds lamb shoulder or chuck
     1   quart lamb or beef stock
     1   pound onions, peeled and diced
     1   pound fresh carrots, scraped and diced
    2½   pounds small potatoes, peeled
     1   rib celery
    2–3 bay leaves
     1   whole clove
         Dash Worcestershire sauce
         Salt and pepper to taste

Cut the lamb into 1-inch cubes. Place in large saucepan and cover with cold water (NO SALT). Bring to a boil and allow to simmer 2–3 minutes. Pour off all the water and thoroughly wash meat in cold water.

Add to the quart of lamb stock the onions, carrots and celery (all diced to 1-inch size), bay leaves and cloves. Bring to a boil and simmer for 5 minutes.

Add the lamb and the small potatoes (whole). Bring to a boil and simmer 25–30 minutes until vegetables are soft and meat is tender. Add a dash of Worcestershire sauce and salt and pepper to taste.

Serve in soup plate and place dumpling (recipe below) on top. Makes 8 portions.

Dumplings

     ½   pound matzoh meal
     1   teaspoon baking powder
     3   eggs, lightly beaten
     ¾   cup milk
     2   tablespoons butter, melted
     1   tablespoon chopped parsley

Mix dry ingredients together. Add eggs, milk and melted butter; mix well. Let stand for 20 minutes.

Shape into small ovals of 1½ inches and poach in lamb broth until tender, 12 to 15 minutes. Garnish each bowl of stew with a dumpling.

Serve in soup bowl.

CHARLEY O'S DEEP-DISH HOT APPLE PIE

Juice from 1 lemon
Juice from 1 orange
1   teaspoon vanilla extract
4   cups white cooking wine
1   teaspoon cinnamon
2   cups sugar
1   cup raisins
6   pounds apples, peeled and sliced thickly
1   loaf white bread, unsliced, *at least two days old*
    Melted butter (approximately ¾ pound)

Mix the lemon juice, orange juice, vanilla, wine and cinnamon in a large saucepan. Add the sugar and stir well. Bring the liquid to a boil and cook for 5 minutes at medium heat. Then remove from the fire and set aside.

In a separate saucepan steam the raisins in water to cover for 15 minutes. Add the sliced apples and mix together lightly. Be sure NOT TO CRUSH the apples.

Next, pour the liquid from the first saucepan over the apple mixture and slowly bring to a boil. Once the mixture starts to boil, remove from heat immediately.

Separate the sauce from the apples and raisins by pouring the mixture through a strainer. Do not press apples through the strainer but keep separate from the liquid. Put the liquid into a saucepan and reduce this sauce to about ¼ of its original volume. This will take approximately 30 minutes.

Pour reduced sauce back over the apples and allow to stand for at least 12 hours.

Preparation of Individual Pies:

Cut the loaf of stale white bread into thin slices. You will need a small circular piece of bread for the bottom and a slightly larger circular piece for the top of each pie. Cut the remaining slices into oblong shapes. These oblong strips will form the side crust for each pie.

Now take the small circular piece of bread and dip in the melted butter and place in the bottom of a 5-inch individual casserole. Repeat this step for all 12 pies.

One strip at a time, dip the oblong pieces in the melted butter and place around the inside of each deep dish. Make sure that each individual strip overlaps the previous strip by approximately ½ inch. The strips of bread should cover completely the sides of the dish.

Now fill each dish to its top with the apple mixture.

Dip the larger circular piece of bread in the melted butter and place on top of each pie.

Bake in a preheated oven at 350° F. for 20 minutes. Remove from the oven and let stand until hot apple pie is ready to serve, or serve immediately by turning each dish upside down on individual serving platter. Place platter under broiler for a few minutes until top crust is brown and crisp. Serve hot, with vanilla sauce, heavy cream or ice cream.

Makes 12 individual pies.

PART III

German and Middle European Food

Chapter VIII

GERMAN AND AUSTRIAN FOOD

≈≈≈≈≈≈≈≈≈≈≈≈≈≈≈≈≈≈≈≈≈≈≈≈≈

Restaurants and Recipes

THE GERMANS were among the first groups, after the Founding Fathers from Holland and Great Britain, to come to the United States in large numbers. They began to emigrate after the revolution of 1848 shook Germany, and in less than 20 years they were the largest non-English-speaking minority in New York.

More quickly than most groups, the Germans took on American ways with little difficulty. But they still managed to retain the flavor of their native land. By 1900 they had begun to leave the Lower East Side, where they had first settled, and move north to Yorkville. This area, centering around 86th Street and Third Avenue, is still the nucleus of the nearly 500,000 Germans living in New York today. Even those Germans who have moved away come back on weekends to shop in the German food stores, eat in German restaurants and *Konditoreien,* buy German books and records and take in a German film.

While the largest Austrian move to the United States occurred well after the Germans had arrived in the millions, the ties of language and cuisine kept the two people close. New York has almost a quarter million Austrians, many of them

Marzipan, fruits and vegetables can be bought in this little shop on East 86th Street in the heart of the German district of uptown New York.

from lands of the old Austro-Hungarian Empire that are no longer part of Austria. The non-Jewish Austrians tend to live, shop and eat in the same neighborhoods as the Germans. Like the Germans, they've had relatively little trouble adjusting to American ways; at the same time, like the Germans, they have kept their own cuisine, their own personal customs and their own identity.

GERMAN FOOD

If ever a cuisine was devised to make the average male completely happy, it is German. Who else but the German cook makes such superb pot roast, complete with dumplings and rich gravy, or such spicy stuffed pork chops served with the crisp contrast of sauerkraut and the bland creaminess of the world's best potato pancakes?

But let us not stop at a potato pancake. The real triumph of German gastronomy is the delicatessen, a German word, a German idea and a German feast. Dozens of sausages, hot or cold, mustards as bland as cream or so hot only the dedicated could stand them; pickles, every kind of pickle; and pickled beets, pickled cucumbers, pickled cabbage, pickled pigs' feet, and bread—pumpernickel and rye are just starters.

Maybe the delicatessen began because German cooking is complicated. Frau Wistersnickel, or whoever, had to have a night or two off. But no one can live forever on delicatessen fare; and for those moments when you feel like cooking—and eating—there's the wonderfully good German meal. Whether the choice is sauerbraten, with no less than 17 ingredients, which you must start at least four days in advance, or baked pigs' knuckles in red wine with *Winekraut* (easy, there are only 16 ingredients), nothing will bring you richer rewards in the form of devotion from husbands, brothers, fathers, uncles or beaux.

What's more, with German food there's German beer. It's hard to say which came first. Like the chicken and the egg, was there in the beginning the fantastically good beer and then a cuisine invented to go with it, or did someone decide to create a beverage that would complement the sausage and sauerbraten to perfection? No matter, the fact remains that beer, real German beer, whether *Helles* (light) or *Dunkels* (dark), is what's needed with German food.

There's much more to be said on the subject than these few lines (we have only skimmed the surface), but no one can touch on German food without a concluding word on strudel—the queen of pastries. Air-light, fruit-filled and swathed in whipped cream, it remains the crowning touch to a menu that may not be exactly calorie-conscious but leaves little doubt that one has eaten superbly well.

LUCHOW'S

110 East 14th Street   *GR 7-4860*

Luchow's has been a landmark for almost 90 years, and this venerable great hall of *Gemütlichkeit* still reigns as the most revered German restaurant in town.

Whenever there's a festival at Luchow's—and there is almost always a festival at Luchow's—the German band goes oom-pah-pah and flags swing from the high ceiling. When there is no festival in action, the scene is only slightly more sedate and the din only a few decibels less.

The food is usually excellent and always served in enormous portions; there's cold beer, the aura of the past, the celebrities, the *Gemütlichkeit*.

Luchow's is open every day from 11:00 A.M. to midnight.

NATUR SCHNITZEL

(Veal Cutlet with Imported Steinpilzen)

4	veal cutlets (about 6 ounces each)
	Salt and pepper
	Flour
¼	pound (1 stick) butter or margarine
1	cup chicken stock or bouillon
2	shallots, peeled and chopped fine

Central Park's Children's Zoo—a great place for little kids—and big kids, too.

2   tablespoons butter or margarine
1   can (No. 2) imported Limousin mushrooms (*Steinpilzen*),
     drained and sliced
2   tablespoons chopped chives

Pound cutlets thin; season with salt and pepper; dip lightly in flour. In large skillet, melt ¼ pound butter and sauté cutlets until golden on both sides. Remove cutlets and keep warm. Add chicken broth to hot skillet, scraping bottom of pan well to loosen brown bits. Cook over medium heat, stirring frequently, until liquid is reduced by ½. Meanwhile, in separate skillet sauté shallots in 2 tablespoons butter until transparent. Add mushrooms; cook 3–4 minutes longer.

To serve, cover cutlets with shallot-mushroom mixture, strain gravy over top and sprinkle with chopped chives. Serve with white asparagus tips and pan-roasted potatoes.

Serves 4.

SAUERBRATEN
(German Pot Roast)

3   pounds round steak
1   teaspoon salt
½   teaspoon pepper
1   large clove garlic, crushed
½   cup sliced onion
1   carrot, peeled and sliced
1   rib celery, chopped
1   teaspoon salt
½   teaspoon whole peppercorns
2   bay leaves
1   cup red wine
1   cup red wine vinegar
2   tablespoons shortening
5   tablespoons butter
4   tablespoons all-purpose flour
3   tablespoons sugar
8   gingersnaps, crushed

Rub steak on both sides with salt, pepper and garlic; place in glass or enamelware utensil. Combine onions, carrot, celery, 1 teaspoon salt, peppercorns and bay leaves; distribute over meat. Add wine, vinegar and enough water to completely cover meat.

Cover tightly and marinate in refrigerator 4 to 6 days, turning once a day.

Remove meat from marinade and pat dry with paper toweling, reserving marinade. In large skillet or Dutch oven brown meat well on both sides in combined shortening and 1 tablespoon butter. Drain off excess drippings. Pour marinade (with vegetables) over meat and bring to boil. Cover tightly and simmer until fork-tender (about 3 hours). Meanwhile, in separate saucepan or skillet melt remaining 4 tablespoons butter; blend in flour and sugar. Cook over medium heat, stirring constantly, until rich golden brown. Remove meat from pan; keep hot. Strain cooking liquid, forcing as much as possible of solids through sieve, and gradually blend into browned flour mixture. Cook and stir until smooth; stir in gingersnaps and cook, stirring constantly, until thickened. Strain through cheesecloth or fine sieve.

Serve with thinly sliced beef. Accompany sauerbraten with potato dumplings and red cabbage.

Serves 6.

LUCHOW'S FLAMING PANCAKE WITH IMPORTED LINGONBERRIES

1½	cups sifted all-purpose flour
1	tablespoon sugar
½	teaspoon salt
4	large eggs
2½	cups milk
2	tablespoons butter, melted
	Additional butter for skillet
	Granulated sugar
	Lemon juice
2	jars (14 ounces each) imported Swedish lingonberries
	Cinnamon-sugar mixture
1	cup kirschwasser, slightly warmed (or Jamaica rum if preferred)

Sift together flour, sugar and salt. In large mixing bowl beat eggs thoroughly; beat in milk. Gradually beat in flour mixture and melted butter; beat 5 minutes. Strain through cheesecloth or fine sieve.

For each pancake: Melt enough butter in a 10-inch omelet

pan, crepe pan or skillet to coat bottom and sides. When hot enough to sizzle a few drops of water, ladle 4 to 5 tablespoons batter into pan as evenly as possible, tipping pan to spread batter thinly. Bake over medium to high heat about 2 minutes, or until lightly browned. Turn, bake other side. Slip out onto hot serving platter. Sprinkle with sugar and lemon juice and spread thickly with about ⅓ cup lingonberries. Roll both sides up onto center. Sprinkle generously with cinnamon-sugar mixture; pour over about 2 tablespoons *warmed* kirschwasser and ignite. Serve immediately. Repeat process until all batter is used.

Makes 6–8 large or 12–14 small pancakes.

BAKED PIG'S KNUCKLES IN RED WINE SAUCE OVER WINEKRAUT

4	pig's knuckles
1	small onion
6	whole peppercorns
1	carrot, sliced
2	bay leaves
1	quart sauerkraut
½	cup sliced onion
2	tablespoons bacon drippings
2	medium apples, peeled, cored and sliced
1½	cups white wine
½	cup beef consommé (about)
1	teaspoon light brown sugar
2	shallots, finely chopped
2	tablespoons butter
1	tablespoon all-purpose flour
1	cup red wine
	Salt and pepper to taste

To prepare pig's knuckles: In deep saucepan cover knuckles with salted water. Add onions, peppercorns, carrot and bay leaves. Cover and boil 2½ to 3 hours or until tender.

To prepare winekraut: Drain sauerkraut slightly. In large skillet sauté onion in bacon drippings until transparent; stir in

Onion rolls, smoked fish, barrels of sauerkraut, dill pickles and green tomatoes in the appetizer store Russ & Daughters on East Houston Street in New York's Lower East Side.

sauerkraut, apples, white wine and enough consommé to cover kraut. Cook, uncovered, over low heat 30 minutes, stirring frequently. Stir in brown sugar. Cover and bake at 325° F. 30 minutes. Keep warm.

To prepare red wine sauce: In small saucepan sauté shallots in butter until tender. Gradually blend in flour and allow to brown, stirring constantly. Gradually stir in red wine; simmer over low heat 10 minutes. Correct seasoning with salt and pepper to taste.

To assemble: Place hot winekraut in baking utensil. Drain pigs' knuckles and arrange over winekraut. Cover with red wine sauce and brown in preheated 425° F. oven. Serve with mashed potatoes.

Serves 4 to 6.

SCHWARZWALDER PFIFFERLINGE IN DILL SAUCE

(Imported Black Forest Mushrooms in Dill Sauce)

1	can (16 ounces) imported Black Forest mushrooms (*Pfifferlinge*)
1	small onion, finely chopped
1	stick butter (¼ pound)
1	rounded tablespoon all-purpose flour
½	teaspoon beef extract (Bovril)
2	tablespoons finely chopped fresh dill or 1 tablespoon dried dill weed (be sure jar is fresh stock)
	Salt and pepper to taste

Drain mushrooms, reserving ⅔ cup liquid (or as much as possible, adding water or chicken stock to make ⅔ cup total). In medium-sized skillet sauté mushrooms and onion in butter until onion is nearly tender and transparent. Blend in flour and beef extract. Gradually stir in reserved mushroom liquid; simmer gently 15 minutes, stirring frequently. Stir in sour cream, dill, salt and pepper to taste, but DO NOT BOIL.

Serve with boiled potatoes or over wild rice.

Serves 4 to 6.

KARTOFFEL KLOSSE
(Potato Dumplings)

9   medium Idaho potatoes (about 3 pounds), cooked very tender and mashed very smooth
3   egg yolks, well beaten
3   tablespoons cornstarch
3   tablespoons all-purpose flour
1½   teaspoons salt
½   teaspoon pepper
¼   teaspoon nutmeg
1   cup toasted white bread cubes (or packaged croutons)
     Flour for rolling
2   tablespoons butter, melted
½   cup dry bread crumbs (unseasoned)

In large bowl beat egg yolks into mashed potatoes. Gradually beat in cornstarch, flour, salt, pepper and nutmeg. Shape into dumplings (about 2 inches in diameter); place 2 or 3 bread cubes in center of each dumpling. Roll each dumpling lightly in flour. Cook, covered, in deep boiling water 10 to 15 minutes or until slightly puffed and set. Remove with slotted spoon; drain on absorbent paper and keep hot. While dumplings are cooking, blend melted butter and bread crumbs together; spoon over dumplings and serve with sauerbraten or any German meat dish.

Makes about 30 2-inch-diameter dumplings.

LUCHOW'S WIENER SCHNITZEL
(Luchow's Veal Cutlet)

4   veal cutlets (7 ounces each)
     Salt and pepper to taste
     All-purpose flour for dredging
2   eggs, well beaten
     Dry bread crumbs (unseasoned)
1   stick butter (¼ pound)
     Lemon wedges
     Parsley sprigs

Pound cutlets very thin (or have butcher do this before delivery). Season to taste with salt and pepper. Dredge lightly in

KATZ's on Delancey Street on the Lower East Side is the place to go

when you want Jewish salami and pastrami and all the rest of it.

flour, then dip in egg, then dredge in bread crumbs. Allow to "set" for about 10 minutes. In large skillet melt butter; add cutlets and sauté over medium to low heat 4 to 5 minutes per side or until golden brown. Place on hot serving platter and garnish with lemon wedge and parsley. Serve immediately.

Serves 4.

Variation: Schnitzel Holstein

Place 1 fried egg on top each veal cutlet. Garnish with 4 anchovy filets, a few sliced beets and tiny gherkin pickles. Serve with German fried potatoes.

NEW AUSTRIAN VILLAGE RESTAURANT

314 East 86th Street   *734-9247*

Mary and Bill Goldschmidt are from Vienna, and the cuisine is ample proof of their ancestry. Opened fourteen years ago, the New Austrian is not exactly new, but the food makes up for whatever may be lacking in the decor.

The restaurant is open from noon to 10:00 P.M. Closed Tuesday.

APFELKUCHEN

	Short dough (see below)
4	tart apples, peeled, cored and sliced
½	cup raisins
¾	cup sugar
½	teaspoon cinnamon
¼	teaspoon nutmeg
¼	cup water ·
½	cup heavy cream
2	tablespoons powdered or extra-fine granulated sugar

Bake short dough for 15 minutes in preheated (375° F.) oven. Mix apples with raisins, sugar, spices and water in a heavy saucepan. Cook over moderate heat until apples are barely tender and syrup has thickened. Apples should still be firm enough to hold their shape. Fill short-dough pastry with apple mixture and bake an additional 15 to 20 minutes at 300° F. Whip cream with powdered sugar and garnish cake with it before serving.

Serves 6-8.

Murbteig
(*Short Dough*)

2	cups sifted flour
½	cup sugar
¾	cup butter, very cold
2	egg yolks, cold
	Grated rind of 1 lemon

Sift sugar and flour together into large mixing bowl and place in freezer to chill. Cut butter into small pieces; chill for 15 minutes. Quickly combine all ingredients, working into a smooth ball. Rinse hands with cold water to keep them cool. Roll out ⅔ of dough ¼ inch thick and press gently onto the bottom of a 10-inch round cake pan. Roll out remaining dough into a thick, long roll and press gently around bottom dough to form sides. Bake in a preheated 375° F. oven for 15 minutes or until lightly browned and cake shrinks from sides of pan.

PAPRIKAHENDL
(*Chicken Paprika*)

1	3- to 4-pound frying chicken, cut into serving pieces
2	tablespoons butter
2	tablespoons vegetable oil
3	large shallots, peeled and chopped
2	tablespoons Hungarian sweet paprika
2	large ripe tomatoes, peeled, seeded and chopped
2	tablespoons flour
½	cup sour cream

Wash chicken under cold running water and dry well with paper towels. Heat butter and oil in large, heavy sauté pan. Brown chicken pieces over moderately high heat; remove to a heated platter. Sauté shallots until limp, then return chicken to pan. Add ½ of the paprika and the tomatoes, stir to blend, cover and cook over low heat until chicken is tender, 30 to 45 minutes. Remove chicken, blend in flour and cook, stirring constantly, for 1 or 2 minutes. Lower heat, add sour cream and stir to blend. Return chicken to pan and cook slowly over very low flame until very hot. Do not allow to boil after adding cream.

Serves 6.

Chapter IX

CZECHOSLOVAKIAN FOOD

~~~~~~

Restaurants and Recipes

IN THE EAST 70s, just below the Hungarian neighborhood between First and Second Avenues, there are Czechoslovak restaurants, food stores, bakeries, bookstores, churches, social clubs, benefit organizations and newspapers. And, of course, there are Czechoslovakians. Not all of the city's 58,000 still live in this old neighborhood, but many of them do. And those who have moved away come back often to shop, attend socials and churches, see friends and eat. This is still the best place in the city to get a truly authentic Czechoslovak meal.

CZECHOSLOVAKIAN FOOD

For all their solid, substantial ways the Czechs have a passion for good living. Prague, the mellow gray and gold capital, is studded with theatres and bookshops, music halls and opera houses and, above all, restaurants and cafés. One, in fact, U Fleku, has been serving foaming tankards of beer, fat spicy sausages, sheep's milk cheese, and crusty Czech bread since 1499, just seven years after Columbus discovered America.

179

It's a no-nonsense cuisine of pork and sauerkraut, roast goose and dumplings all washed down with their golden Pilsner, one of the truly great beers of the world. Like all of Middle Europe, the Czechs love their mocha coffee and their meltingly rich pastries. All over Prague one can see the solid housewives and shop workers leisurely enjoying their fragrant coffee, plates piled high with flaky tarts and cream-filled cakes.

But there is more to the Czech food than roasts and sweets. Prague ham is superb and is shipped all over the world; pickles and stewed fruits add spice and variety to almost every dish, and there are marvelous hearty soups. Endless varieties of dumplings and sausages display the Czech knack for a light hand and a good touch with seasonings, and if one tires of the creamy pastries, there is an infinite array of fruit dumplings to cover with sour cream and end the meal in a haze of culinary satisfaction.

The honest flavor and substantial goodness of Czech food has lost little if anything in its translation to New York's shores. While not numerous, the Czechoslovakian restaurants are serious about their cooking and the results leave little to be desired. What's more, though the atmosphere may not, in the best of Czech tradition, be frivolous or gay, there is a satisfying ambience of good will that is perhaps the best of all sauces for the diner.

PRAHA RESTAURANT

1358 First Avenue   *YU 8-3505*

Two generations of the Holechek family have been running this family-style restaurant since 1940. The kitchen crew and the waiters are from Czechoslovakia and the result is honest Czechoslovak food.

Recently remodeled, Praha has a formidable exterior; inside, the main decorative point is a wall mural of seventeenth-century Prague.

The restaurant is open every day from noon to 11:00 P.M.

One of the many interesting churches peppered throughout New York.
This one is on the Upper West Side, near Columbus Avenue.

SAUERKRAUT, PRAHA STYLE

1   pound prepared sauerkraut
     Water as needed
2   large onions, peeled and chopped
¼   cup caraway seeds
¾   cup sugar

Place sauerkraut in a large pot. Fill pot with water, let stand
1 minute, then drain. Repeat. This double rinsing removes
briny taste.

Place sauerkraut in large pot, adding only enough water to
moisten—about ½ cup. Add remaining ingredients, cover and
let cook over very low heat for 2 to 2½ hours, folding over
sauerkraut every half-hour; add water as needed.

Serves 4.

VASATA

339 East 75th Street   *RH 4-9896*

Jaroslav Vasata came to New York from Prague, where he
owned the largest restaurant in Czechoslovakia. His new restaurant in New York is small rather than large, and cozy rather
than grand, but the food and the atmosphere are still authentically Czechoslovakian.

Vasata is open from 5:00 P.M. to 11:00 P.M. and on Sunday
from noon to 10:00 P.M.

BOILED BEEF WITH DILL SAUCE

4-5   pounds beef for boiling
      Water
      Salt
      Soup vegetables

Sauce

1   quart soup stock (more if needed)
2   tablespoons flour mixed in ½ cup cold water
       (more if needed)
1   tablespoon butter

1   teaspoon sugar
1   cup sour cream
½   cup condensed milk
    Juice from ½ lemon
    Sugar
    Salt
½   cup chopped fresh dill

Wash meat, place in boiling water (meat must be covered with water), boil awhile and skim; add salt and vegetables, cover and simmer until meat is done (about 3 hours). Strain soup; ladle about a quart into a sauce pot, add flour mixed well with cold water and beat well with a wire whisk; add butter and sugar and simmer at least ½ hour (the longer it cooks, the better it gets), stirring occasionally. If sauce should get too thick, add more soup stock; if too thin, add more flour mixture. Sauce should have the consistency of heavy syrup before you add the final touches. Before serving, add the sour cream, milk, lemon juice, sugar and salt to taste, and stir well. Heat, but do not boil. Add chopped dill.

Any soup stock left over can be served with thin noodles as beef noodle soup or used as a base for cream soups.

ROAST DUCKLING

1   Long Island duckling, about 5–6 pounds
    Salt
    Caraway seeds
    Pork bones
1   teaspoon cornstarch

Preheat oven to 450° F.

Wash the duckling and rub both outside and inside with salt and caraway seeds. Place the bird in an open roasting pan on a bed of bones, adding cold water to barely cover bottom of pan (more water may be added during cooking, but not much). Roast duckling for about 2½ hours or until tender; while roasting, turn every ½ hour and prick the skin so that all the fat can run out. Baste with pan drippings. When finished, the bird should be golden brown and there should not be any fat under the skin.

Remove duckling from pan. Drain off most of the fat. Add

Whatever cheese you want, they probably have it at Cheeses of the World on Second Avenue, uptown New York.

water to the bones in the pan and scrape sides of pan. Cook in oven for about 15 minutes. Strain gravy into a sauce pot and bring to boil on top of stove. Add cornstarch mixed with some cold water, stirring with a wire whisk until smooth, and simmer 15 minutes. Add salt to taste if necessary; if too salty, add more water.
Serves 4.

TRIPE SOUP

1	pound tripe cut into ¼-inch slices
	Water
2	tablespoons butter
1	small onion, peeled and chopped
2½	tablespoons flour
1	tablespoon sweet paprika
1½	quarts beef stock
2	cloves garlic, crushed
	Ground pepper
	Marjoram
	Salt

Pour cold water over tripe and cook for ½ hour; strain, rinse tripe, cover with salted fresh water and cook until tender. Strain.

In a heavy soup pot fry onions in butter until golden, add flour and paprika, and cook over low heat 5 minutes, stirring often so the paprika does not burn. Pour beef stock over mixture in the soup pot, stir well and cook partly covered for ½ hour. Add tripe and cook another 5 minutes, stirring constantly. If soup is too thick, add more stock or water. Season with pepper, garlic, marjoram and salt to taste.
Serves 6.

BREAD DUMPLINGS

½	loaf stale white bread, diced
2	tablespoons butter
4	cups flour
½	teaspoon salt
1	cup milk
½	cup cold water
3	eggs

Fry diced bread in butter until golden and let cool. Sift flour with salt in a large mixing bowl. Combine milk, water and eggs, and pour mixture slowly into flour, stirring with a large wooden spoon. Then beat dough with the same spoon until very smooth and medium thick. Stir in fried bread and let stand ½ hour. Divide dough into 2 parts. Shape into 2 long dumpling rolls (they look like small loaves of Italian bread) and slip them into boiling salted water. You will need a very large pot for this. Boil 30 minutes, turning once with a wooden spoon. Cut dumplings while hot with a very sharp, thin knife. Slices should be about ½ inch thick. You can steam to reheat if you have any left over.

Serves 6–8.

HUNGARIAN FOOD

~~~~~~

Restaurants and Recipes

THE SOLIDLY entrenched Hungarian community of New York reigns on the southern fringes of Yorkville, around Second Avenue and 79th Street. Like all the little ethnic "cities within the city," the Hungarian area has its own restaurants, food stores, entertainments, churches, newspapers and organizations.

New York's Hungarian population soared to nearly 120,000 after the 1956 insurrection in Hungary caused thousands to flee to the United States. Hungary's loss has meant that some of that country's finest restaurateurs and chefs are now living and working in New York. For New York it means a new spate of restaurants to complement the old, all the goulash and paprikash New Yorkers want to eat, and food stores that supply the spice of life, paprika, imported from Hungary in sweet, medium and hot varieties, just the way it was back home.

HUNGARIAN FOOD

There is a half-joking definition of a Hungarian as "someone who can go into a revolving door after you and come out ahead of you." And it could be true; shrewd, witty, artistic, practical, romantic, intelligent, high-spirited, clever—these are adjectives

A young customer knows a good place to get the real thing in Hungarian

sausages—Second Avenue in the Seventies.

that aptly describe the Hungarian, and they might well be applied to their cuisine.

Varied, interesting and fantastically good, Hungarian food is far more than cabbage and paprika. The reign of the Turks over Hungary for 150 years left a heritage of tropical fruits, nuts, melons and spices. Paprika was introduced by the Turks, and anyone who knows Hungarian food will not doubt that the pashas did indeed leave their imprint on Hungarian kitchens. Later the Hapsburg Austro-Hungarian dynasty, with its intermarriages with the nobility of France and Italy, brought a new refinement to what was admittedly rather crude fare.

Today the gourmet can find bliss in the lavish produce of Hungary's famous plains, its prized beef and pork, its incredible pastry, and happily, because it has crossed the Atlantic, its devoted "labor of love" attitude toward the creation of good food.

The Hungarian cook regards his profession as an art. Succulent roasts, rose-brown with paprika, the lightest noodles, the freshest vegetables and fruits, airy pancakes filled with cottage cheese clouded with sour cream, turkey stuffed with chestnuts, strudels and pastries are everyday products of the Hungarian kitchen—little enough to expect when one realizes that the Hungarian tradition for good eating goes back a long way. Ruszwrwm, a famous coffeehouse in Budapest, is more than 400 years old, and the Pilvax is noted more for its pastries than for the fact the 1848 revolution was plotted there. It would seem you would be in good hands with people who stopped first for coffee and pastry before planning a revolution.

BUDAPEST HUNGARIAN RESTAURANT
1481 Second Avenue *744-9432*

This is now the oldest Hungarian restaurant in the city. Begun by Mrs. Giselle Csaszar 25 years ago, it is still a family affair. The cooking is home-style, and the service is warm and personal. It is doubtful that anyone has ever left the Budapest hungry.

The restaurant is open every day from noon to 10:30 P.M.

TŐLTÖTT KÁPOSZTA

(Stuffed Cabbage)

1	large head of cabbage with plenty of good unbroken green leaves
1	cup water
3	tablespoons oil
1	medium onion, chopped
1	pound lean beef, ground
¼	pound lean pork, ground
1	cup cooked rice
1	egg, beaten
½	teaspoon salt
1	teaspoon paprika
1	cup veal or beef stock
½	cup sour cream

Carefully separate the large outer leaves from the cabbage, taking care not to break them. You will need 2 leaves for each serving. Wash well under cold running water. Reserve inner portion of cabbage for salad. Place the leaves in a large, heavy saucepan; add water, cover and steam for 5 minutes. Drain. In a heavy skillet heat the oil and sauté the onion in it until limp but not brown, add the beef and the pork, and continue to cook over moderate heat, stirring and breaking up the meat into small particles until it is no longer pink. Remove from heat and add cooked rice, egg and seasonings. Stir well to blend.

Stuff cabbage leaves with meat mixture and place seam side down in an ovenproof casserole. Rolls should be packed tightly in casserole to hold their shape. Pour veal or beef stock over rolls, cover and bake in a moderate (350° F.) oven for 1½ hours. Remove rolls to a heated platter. Pour pan juice into a saucepan and simmer until it is reduced to ½ cupful. Stir in sour cream and continue to cook over low heat until very hot. Do not allow to boil after adding cream. Pour over rolls and serve very hot.

Makes about 12 rolls.

A fascinating array of candies and sausages (Kolbasz) at Paprikas

Weiss on Second Avenue.

PALACSINTA

(Pancakes)

   2   cups sifted flour
  ½   teaspoon salt
   5   eggs, separated
  1½   cups milk
   3   tablespoons butter (approximately)
        Raspberry jam
   1   cup sour cream

Combine flour, salt, egg yolks and 1 cup of milk. Beat with
a wooden spoon until smooth, add balance of milk and blend
well. Beat egg whites until stiff but not dry and fold into first
mixture.

Grease a large, flat griddle (or electric skillet) with a little
of the butter and heat until a little water dropped on it immediately boils and evaporates. Pour ¼ cup of batter on the griddle and immediately tilt and rotate so that batter covers the
surface for about an 8-inch cake. Batter will be thin. Cook
over moderately high heat for a moment or two and until fine
bubbles cover the top and cake turns easily. Turn and brown
opposite side. Total cooking time should be no more than 3
minutes. Remove cake to heated platter, spread with raspberry
jam and roll up. Keep warm in low oven until all of the cakes
have been made. Top with sour cream and serve while still
warm.

Makes 8 to 10 cakes.

EVA HUNGARIAN RESTAURANT

1556 Second Avenue   *861-1096*

A marvelous cafeteria-style restaurant, home-style Hungarian
dishes rich with paprika, and of course for dessert those wonderful pastries.

Eva Hungarian Restaurant is open from noon to 11:00 P.M.
Closed Monday.

CHICKEN PAPRIKA

1 2½- to 3-pound chicken, cut into serving pieces
3 tablespoons butter
1 medium onion, peeled and chopped
1 half small green pepper, seeded and chopped
1 tablespoon flour
1 teaspoon salt
½ teaspoon pepper
1½ cups chicken stock
1 cup light cream
2 teaspoons paprika
 Cooked rice

Blot chicken thoroughly dry with paper towels. Heat butter in a large heavy skillet. Add chicken pieces and cook, turning them with a wooden spoon until meat begins to firm. Push chicken to one side of pan. Add onion and green pepper and cook, stirring two to three minutes. Cover pan and cook for a few minutes longer. Sprinkle chicken pieces with flour, salt and pepper. Stir and turn chicken pieces for one to two minutes. Add stock, cover and let simmer for thirty minutes, or until chicken is tender. Stir in cream and paprika and cook over low heat until sauce is thick and hot. Do not allow to boil after adding cream. Serve over just cooked hot rice.

Serves 4.

PART IV

Russian Food

Chapter XI

RUSSIAN FOOD

〜〜〜〜〜〜〜〜〜〜〜〜〜〜〜〜〜〜〜〜〜〜〜〜〜〜〜〜〜〜

Restaurants and Recipes

OF ALL THE people in New York, perhaps the Russians are the hardest to define. At least 700,000 people in New York have a Russian heritage, and this does not count the Ukrainians. But a majority of this number are Yiddish-speaking Jews with no cultural ties to the Russians, another 100,000 are Slavic, a small number are Russian Moslems of Tartar ancestry, and then there are the White Russians, émigrés from the Bolshevik Revolution. They all keep separate from one another. Needless to say, there are very few recent immigrants.

It is almost as hard to define a markedly Russian area in the city. There is an old Russian neighborhood around East 14th Street, close to the Ukrainian and Polish communities. But there are also many Russians on the Upper West Side near Broadway and 160th Street, as well as in other areas of the city.

Certainly their restaurants and nightclubs, many of which tend to open and close with predictable rapidity, are spread, without obvious pattern, throughout the city. But those which have been in the city a long time, such as the Russian Tea Room and Russian Bear, are among the liveliest, most enjoyable places in town.

Symbol of the USSR at the United Nations, with the ultra-elegant UN Plaza Apartments in the background.

RUSSIAN BEAR

139 East 56th Street   *355-9080*

This is a supper club with a menu of Russian dishes served by Russian waiters and accompanied by a strolling Russian gypsy orchestra.

Present owners Matislav and Titania Tarwid say the Russian Bear is the oldest Russian restaurant in the United States. It opened its first door, several addresses ago, in 1908.

Russian Bear is open every night from 5:00 P.M. to 3:00 A.M.

CREME A LA RUSSE

1½	cups water
1	package strawberry gelatin
1	package unflavored gelatin
2	tablespoons sugar
1	cup water
4	cups heavy cream
1	cup powdered sugar
1	teaspoon vanilla
1	cup sliced fresh strawberries
	Whole strawberries to garnish

Bring the 1½ cups water to a full boil and pour over strawberry gelatin in large mixing bowl. Stir until gelatin dissolves. Pour into a shallow square pan and refrigerate until firm. Combine sugar with plain gelatin in mixing bowl. Bring the 1 cup of water to a full boil and pour over mixture. Stir until sugar and gelatin have dissolved. Let stand until just warm.

Beat cream until thick. Fold in powdered sugar and vanilla extract, then gently fold in warm gelatin. Add sliced strawberries and pour over chilled strawberry gelatin. Refrigerate until cream mixture is firm. Garnish with whole strawberries just before serving.

Serves 12.

BORSCH MALOROSSIYSKIY
(Russian Vegetable Soup)

1   large mild (purple) onion
1   rib celery
3   carrots, scraped
1   small green pepper, seeded
2   medium beets, peeled
1   small turnip, peeled
2   tablespoons vegetable oil
8   cups clear rich beef stock, free of all fat
¼   small head cabbage, chopped
2   medium tomatoes, peeled, seeded and chopped
4   tablespoons tomato puree
5   bay leaves
1   crisp tart apple
    Julienne-style strips of boiled beef (optional)
    Sour cream
    Chopped fresh dill

Peel onion, cut into slices. Cut slices into narrow strips. Cut celery, carrots, green pepper, beets and turnips into julienne-style strips. Sauté all vegetables in oil until they begin to soften—about 10 minutes.

Heat stock until boiling, add sautéed vegetables and cabbage, lower heat and let simmer very gently for 20 minutes. Add tomatoes, tomato puree and bay leaf. Peel and cut apple into julienne strips. Add to soup and cook a final 10 minutes.

Ladle into soup bowls and add, if desired, a few strips of boiled beef to each serving. Top each with a teaspoon of sour cream, sprinkle with fresh dill, and serve at once.

Serves 12.

BREAST OF CHICKEN A LA KIEV

3   chicken breasts, skinned, boned and halved
⅓   pound sweet butter
1   cup flour
1   teaspoon salt
2   egg yolks beaten with 2 tablespoons water
2   cups fine dry bread crumbs
    Oil for frying

Place each half of chicken breast between waxed paper and pound with a meat mallet until thin as veal scallopini.

Soften the butter, divide into 6 portions, then shape each portion into a small "finger." Place, not touching, on foil and refrigerate until firm.

Place a finger of butter in the center of each flattened half of chicken breast, then roll up, tucking end of breast under so that butter is completely encased. Roll each breast first in flour mixed with salt, then in beaten egg yolk and finally in bread crumbs. Again dip in egg, then roll in bread crumbs. Place on wire rack in refrigerator until coating has set, 10 to 15 minutes.

Fill a large, heavy skillet with oil to about 3 inches of rim and heat to 475° F. on deep-frying thermometer. Fry 2 breasts at a time for 5 to 6 minutes. Remove from oil with a slotted spoon and drain briefly on paper toweling.

Serve on bed of rice; garnish if desired with sour cream or thick white sauce.

Serves 6.

RUSSIAN TEA ROOM

150 West 57th Street   *CO 5-0947*

The Russian Tea Room, which hasn't been a tea room since its infancy in the 1920s, likes the shabby gentility of its European restaurant atmosphere. So do hordes of faithfuls, both known and unknown. Dancers Nureyev and Markova, actresses Marlene Dietrich and Maureen Stapleton, the Burtons, the Belafontes, to name a very few, come here to dine among the samovars, the gold tinsel and the aged concert posters against dark green walls.

The Russian Tea Room is open every day from noon to 12:30 A.M.

ROSZOLNICK SOUP

    1   large onion
    2   carrots
    2   white parsley roots

Two bakers at work doing their daily making of bialies on Grand Street, New York's Lower East Side.

2   ribs celery
2   large potatoes
1   quart milk
½   pint sour cream
2   tablespoons flour
2   quarts beef stock
2   dill pickles (chopped) with pickle juice (to taste)

Peel and cut up vegetables and boil for 20 minutes in salted water to cover. Drain and set aside. Combine milk and sour cream. Mix flour with small amount of liquid and add to milk and cream. Cook over low heat until steamy hot. Add beef stock and vegetables, cut dill pickles and juice to flavor. Bring to a boil and then simmer for 20 minutes.

Serves 4 to 6.

PART V

Greek and Near and Middle Eastern Food

Chapter XII

GREEK FOOD

〰〰〰〰〰〰〰〰〰〰〰〰〰〰〰〰〰〰〰〰〰〰

Restaurants and Recipes

ABOUT 100 years ago, it's been reported, there were exactly 119 Greeks in New York. Today there are over 57,000. And according to the latest figures, there is still a sizable number arriving yearly.

In the early days the Greeks settled along Eighth Avenue between 14th and 45th Streets, with the heaviest concentration from the Twenties to the Forties. Today, although many of them have moved to other parts of the city, and accordingly, Greek restaurants have opened wherever Greeks are, this is still the neighborhood for the largest collection of Greek restaurants, nightclubs, food stores and bakeries. Here you'll find Greek newspapers, Greek window signs, and cinemas showing Greek films, and in the evening you'll hear the wail of the bouzouki, the slap of the tsamiko, the passionate beat of Greek music.

Outwardly the clubs and restaurants bear little resemblance to their Athenian counterparts. Inside it's a different matter. The owners are Greeks, the chefs seldom speak anything but Greek, and the decor, although rarely great, is a frankly sentimental reminiscence of that starkly beautiful country on the Aegean. It's obvious that a Greek never forgets Greece. Neither

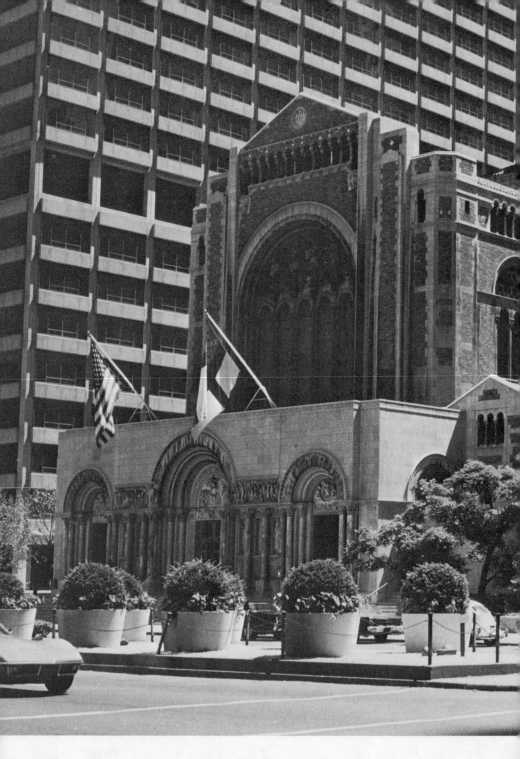

St. Bartholomew's at 50th Street and Park Avenue, one of the most

beautiful churches in New York.

do the diners after they've eaten in one of these neighborhood restaurants, even if they've never been to Greece.

GREEK FOOD

Classic white sauce was not, as one might suppose, a French invention; nor was it Italian. It was devised by Orion, the kitchen sage of ancient Greece. What's more, brown sauce, which we know today as sauce espagñole, was the creation of Lampriadas, another inspired Greek of the same era. Greeks discovered that oysters were edible and good, that onions could be cultivated; furthermore, they baked the first pastry.

With a heritage like that and a sun-washed land of oranges and sweet lemons, almonds and grapes, honey and thyme, plus gentle fields that produce the finest lamb, surrounded by blue crystal seas of fresh fish of every description, it's little wonder that Greeks are natural gourmets and the best of restaurateurs.

Greeks love good food, and more often than not lunch or dinner will consist of several courses: three or four appetizers, a soup, fish, roast meat or poultry, two or three vegetables, salad, cheese, dessert and coffee. With drinks there's always a plate of cheese, olives and meat-filled pastries, for few Greeks will drink without eating. And of course there are all kinds of honey-sweet pastries to have with coffee in the late afternoon.

An artist with seasoning, the Greek cook uses tomatoes, onions, garlic, parsley, oregano, thyme and parsley with a practiced hand. Imaginative and inventive, he will stuff a turkey with chestnuts, prunes, pignolia nuts and raisins; make a casserole of lamb and artichokes; create an airy soufflé with ground lamb and zucchini. And who else but a Greek would have devised avgolemono syrup, that fresh-tasting blend of chicken stock, eggs and lemon?

New York has more than its share of fine Greek restaurants. Time and space have allowed only a few here, but no matter which one you choose, you will doubtless "dine like a god" on one of civilization's oldest and most interesting cuisines.

HELLENIC PALACE
250 West 27th Street   *246-5266*

The colors at the Hellenic Palace are the clear blue of Greece, the luminescent white of marble ruins and that powdery, pinkish red that, seen anywhere in the world, brings back memories of the Mediterranean and pristine light.

The Kletsidis family combines their talents to cook and to manage this gem of a restaurant. And those talents are rather mighty, both in the robust strength of the kitchen and in the engaging hospitality of the dining room.

Hellenic Palace is open from 11:00 A.M. to midnight and on Sunday from 4:00 P.M. to midnight. Closed Monday.

TARAMASALATA
(Fish Roe Dip)

1	8-ounce jar of red caviar
1	small onion, peeled and finely minced
8	to 9 slices firm white bread, Greek, Italian or French, crust removed
1	to 1½ cups olive oil
	Juice from 2 or 3 lemons

Mash caviar and add onion. Dip each slice of bread in water, quickly squeezing out any excess water.

Place bread in a large bowl. Add caviar and onion mixture and beat until blended and smooth. Add olive oil and lemon juice alternately a little at a time, beating well after each addition. Continue to beat until mixture is creamy smooth.

Serve as a dip with crackers or spread on small fingers of Greek bread.

Makes 1½ to 2 cups.

SKORDALIA
(Garlic and Potato Sauce)

4	large potatoes
6–7	cloves garlic, peeled
½	to 1 cup olive oil

Making trays of Greek pastry, such as the honey-filled baklava, at

the Colossus in Astoria, Queens.

2   to 3 tablespoons white wine vinegar
      Salt
      Pepper

Place potatoes in water to cover and cook until tender. Drain and peel.

Crush garlic with pestle in a large bowl. Add potatoes and mash until smooth. Add oil and vinegar alternately in small amounts, blending and then whipping potatoes after each addition. Season to taste with salt and pepper. Serve over baked or broiled fish, or with beets or eggplant.

Makes about 2 cups.

SALATA
(Green Salad)

1   clove garlic, peeled and cut in half
2   cups greens—lettuce, chicory, escarole, romaine, endive
         sections—torn into bite-size pieces
1   large tomato
1   large cucumber, peeled and chopped
      Small bunch parsley, chopped
1   small can anchovies
1   small jar Greek black olives
¼   pound feta cheese, cubed
1   tablespoon lemon juice
3   tablespoons olive oil
      Salt
      Pepper
      Oregano
      Dried mint leaves or chopped fresh mint leaves

Rub a large wooden salad bowl with the garlic. Add greens and place in refrigerator. Plunge tomato into boiling water for a half-minute, then hold under running water and strip off skin. Cut in half and gently squeeze out seeds. Cut into narrow strips. Add tomato strips, cucumber, parsley, anchovies, olives and cheese to greens. Combine lemon juice and olive oil; beat until mixture is frothy. Pour over salad and toss until well blended. Season lightly with salt and pepper. Add a sprinkling of oregano and mint. Toss again and serve.

Serves 4.

DIONYSOS RESTAURANT

304 East 48th Street   *758-8240*

Whitewashed walls, polished gray slate floors and a fresco of Greek tiles form the background for this authentic Greek restaurant. The Greek chef is obviously skilled and the service is swift and attentive.

Dionysos serves lunch from noon to 3:00 P.M. and dinner from 5:00 P.M. until dawn. Closed Sunday.

SAGANAKI

(Melted Cheese)

1	pound kefalotiri, kasseri or feta cheese
1/4	pound butter, melted
	Juice from 1 large lemon
	Paprika

Cut cheese into slices 1/4 inch thick and spread each slice with melted butter. Place in long, shallow pan under direct broiler heat until cheese begins to melt. Transfer to hot oven for 1 to 2 minutes. Sprinkle with lemon juice and paprika. Cut into bite-size pieces and serve immediately.

Serves 6–8 as a cocktail hors d'oeuvre.

SPANAKOTIROPITA

(Spinach Squares)

2	pounds spinach
1	small onion, finely chopped
3	tablespoons olive oil
1	pound feta cheese, crumbled
2	eggs, beaten
	Salt
	Pepper
1/2	pound phyllo pastry sheets
1/4	pound melted and cooled butter

Wash spinach under cold running water.
Fill a large pot with water and bring to a full boil. Add

*You can't get fresher fish in New York than to buy it right off the boats
as they come in with their day's catch at Brooklyn's Sheepshead Bay.*

spinach and cook 1 to 2 minutes. Drain into colander, cool and chop.

Sauté onion in olive oil until soft. Add spinach and cook, stirring gently, for 1 minute. Remove from heat and cool. Add crumbled cheese and eggs. Season lightly with salt and pepper.

Place 6 layers of phyllo pastry sheets in an 11-by-14-by-2-inch buttered pan and brush each sheet of pastry with melted butter after it is added. Add spinach mixture and top with 6 layers of phyllo pastry sheets, again brushing each sheet with melted butter.

Place in a preheated 350° F. oven and bake 30 minutes or until crust is golden brown. Cut into small squares and spear each square with a cocktail pick to hold together.

NOTE: Keep phyllo pastry sheets covered with a damp cloth while preparing spanakotiropita.

Makes about 16 squares.

THE ATHENIAN RESTAURANT

709 Eighth Avenue   *CI 5-9966*

Located in a neighborhood of Greek markets and newsstands, the Athenian attracts both Greeks with a yen for the old country and Americans with a yen for tasty food. The walls are muraled with scenes of whitewashed villages on the Aegean, and each night a bouzouki, a guitar and an accordion complete the scene with Greek folk music.

The Athenian is open every day from noon to 1:00 A.M.

KREAS ME MELITZANA
(Lamb with Eggplant)

1½	pounds lean shoulder of lamb, cut into 1-inch cubes
	Flour
2	tablespoons butter
1	tablespoon oil (more as needed)
1	large onion, peeled and chopped
3	large ripe tomatoes, chopped
½	cup water

1 bay leaf
  Salt
  Pepper
1 large eggplant
1 clove garlic, peeled and chopped
2 teaspoons tomato paste

Pat lamb cubes dry with paper toweling. Dredge lightly with flour. Shake off excess flour.

Heat one tablespoon of butter with the oil in a large heavy skillet. Add meat, a few pieces at a time, and brown well on all sides. Add more oil as needed. Remove meat when browned with a slotted spoon and set aside. Add second tablespoon of butter to the skillet. When heated add onion and sauté until limp. Return meat to skillet. Add chopped tomatoes, water and bay leaf. Season lightly with salt and pepper. Bring to full boil, then lower heat and simmer for one hour. Peel eggplant and cut into 2-inch cubes. Add eggplant, garlic and tomato paste to skillet. Stir to blend. Cover and cook until vegetables and meat are tender—about thirty minutes. Correct seasoning with additional salt as needed.

Serves 4–6.

Chapter XIII

NEAR AND MIDDLE EASTERN FOOD

Restaurants and Recipes

ARMENIANS, Lebanese, Syrians, Egyptians—the people of the complex Near and Middle East whose histories are the beginning of us all, whose boundaries have, through the thousands of years of their existence, shifted, crept, advanced, retreated. Change has been the only consistent factor in their culture, with perhaps two exceptions: language and cuisine. And even they have changed as people absorbed each other's tastes and characteristics. Today the foods of all the countries of the Middle East, while they are essentially what they were in Biblical days, are intermingled with each other.

In New York there are about 30,000 Armenians and perhaps another 30,000 Arabic-speaking people from Lebanon, Syria and neighboring countries.

Once, the neighborhood of Third and Lexington Avenues in the Twenties was home for many of these people, especially the Armenians. Today many of the people and restaurants have moved away, but this is still the best area in Manhattan to find a cluster of good Middle Eastern food stores and eating places.

The food stores and restaurants are aromatic with allspice and

The promenade along Brooklyn Heights waterfront.

cumin, pine nuts and mint. There are bins of eggplants and artichokes. There are butcheries for lamb, bakeries for phyllo and pita. There are jars of honey and bottles of sesame oil, sacks of wheat and bags of chick-peas, tins of grape leaves and tubs of homemade yogurt.

THE CAMEL'S HUMP

130 West 3rd Street   *674-9417*

Next time you begin dreaming of an Arabian night, head for this delightful Middle Eastern restaurant in Greenwich Village. The cooking is predominantly Lebanese with a heady mixture of Syrian, Egyptian, Armenian and Greek. And if you wonder where Syria ends and Egypt begins on the menu, owner Robert Kanatous will be happy to show you.

The Camel's Hump is open every day from 4:00 P.M. to 3:00 A.M.

HUMMUS BI TAHINI
(Chick-Pea Sauce or Dip)

1	cup dried chick-peas
½	cup *tahini*
⅓	cup lemon juice (more if desired)
2	cloves garlic, peeled and finely minced
3¼	teaspoons salt (more if desired)
	Chopped parsley

Place peas in a large pot; cover with water and let soak 12 hours or overnight. Drain, cover with fresh water and place over medium heat. Let simmer until tender, 3 to 4 hours. Drain and cool. Combine with remaining ingredients except parsley.

Place half of mixture in electric blender until smooth. Repeat with remaining half of mixture. Adjust seasoning if desired with additional lemon juice and salt.

Chill thoroughly before serving. Serve as a dip with small cubes of Arabic bread or serve as an accompaniment to main-course meat dishes.

About 2¼ cups sauce or dip.

BOUZA BI HALEEB

(Milk Ice Cream)

4   cups milk
½   teaspoon cornstarch
1¾ cups sugar
½   teaspoon gum arabic
1   teaspoon orange flower water
1   teaspoon grated orange rind
1   cup chopped pistachio nuts
1   small can mandarin orange sections

Pour 1 cup of milk over the cornstarch and stir until blended. Combine remaining milk and 1½ cups of the sugar in a saucepan. Stir until sugar has dissolved, then over medium heat cook until boiling point is reached. Add cold milk and cornstarch mixture, stirring constantly as it is added. Place gum arabic in mortar and pulverize with pestle. Mix well with remaining ¼ cup of the sugar. Add to milk mixture and let simmer over low heat for 10 minutes. Stir frequently. Remove from heat; stir in orange flower water and grated orange rind. Pour into refrigerator trays, cover with foil and place in freezer compartment for 30 minutes or until firm. Remove and quickly transfer to a large mixing bowl. Beat with a wire whisk until smooth. Return to freezer for another 30 minutes, then repeat beating and freezing process again. Remove from freezer and place in refrigerator 15 to 20 minutes before serving.

Serve in tall parfait glasses; garnish each serving with mandarin orange sections and sprinkle with chopped pistachio nuts. Serves 6.

LEBANESE BAKLAVA

2   pounds pistachio nuts, finely chopped
½   cup sugar
    Water as needed
1   pound phyllo pastry sheets
1   pound butter, melted and cooled
    Syrup (see below)

Mix finely chopped pistachio nuts with sugar and add just enough water to hold mixture together.

Butter a large baking pan and line it with 5 sheets of phyllo pastry (brushing each layer with melted butter). Spread some of the nut mixture over entire surface. Add 2 buttered pastry sheets and spread evenly with nut mixture. Continue until all nut mixture has been used. Cover with 5 layers of buttered pastry sheets. With a sharp knife cut baklava into diamond-shaped pieces. Bake in a 325° F. preheated oven for 1 hour. Remove from heat and immediately pour hot syrup over surface. Cool before serving.

Serves 6 or makes about 24 small diamond-shaped pieces.

Syrup

1	cup sugar
1	cup honey
2	cups water
1	teaspoon orange flower water
1	teaspoon lemon juice
1	teaspoon rose water

Combine ingredients and bring to boil, lower heat and let simmer for 20 minutes.

NOTE: To prevent drying out, keep phyllo pastry sheets covered with a damp cloth as you work. Remember to spread each sheet of pastry with melted butter after it is added to pan.

KAFTA 'ALA SHEESH

1	pound lamb neck meat
2	tablespoons yogurt
½	teaspoon ground cloves
¼	teaspoon black pepper
¼	teaspoon ground ginger
¼	teaspoon ground cardamom
½	teaspoon salt
¼	cup finely minced onion
¼	cup finely minced parsley
	Olive oil

Grind meat several times through fine blade of meat grinder. Mix well with remaining ingredients except oil, and form into balls the size of an egg. Thread meatballs onto skewers for broiling. Sprinkle with oil. Broil until rare, medium or well done, according to taste, over charcoal or under oven broiler. Turn often.

Heat and split small loaves of Arabic bread. Fill with broiled meatballs. Add a few sautéed onion rings and eat American style—like a hamburger.

Serves 4.

BEIRUT RESTAURANT
43 West 32nd Street   *OX 5-9898*

George Kalovsia, the owner of Beirut, claims that 95 percent of the Arabic population comes to his restaurant. Considering the authenticity of the cuisine, he may be right; certainly here is the place for Arabic food. Crowded at times and somewhat overdecorated, it is still well worth a visit.

The Beirut is open every day from 11:30 A.M. to 11:30 P.M.

MAHSHI WARAK AREESH
(Stuffed Grape Leaves with Rice and Meat)

16	to 20 grape leaves
1½	tablespoons salad oil
1	small onion, finely chopped
½	pound ground beef
1	cup uncooked rice
¼	teaspoon salt
¼	teaspoon pepper
1	teaspoon dried mint
1	cup beef stock or water
1	teaspoon lemon juice

Soak grape leaves overnight in salted water with ½ teaspoon of the salad oil.

Heat remaining tablespoons of oil in a heavy skillet, sauté chopped onion until limp, add ground beef and cook, stirring frequently, over medium heat until brown. Add uncooked rice, salt, pepper and mint. Stir to blend. Drain grape leaves and stuff with meat-rice mixture. Roll tightly and arrange in heavy

A souvlaki bar on MacDougal Street in Greenwich Village.

cast-iron enamelized saucepan. Pack tightly so that rolls will hold together. Press down firmly. Pour beef stock or water over rolls. Cover tightly and cook over low heat for 20 minutes. Add lemon juice and continue to cook, covered, for an additional 25 minutes. Serve plain or covered with yogurt.

Serves 4.

TZITZIKI
(Cucumber and Yogurt Dip)

1 clove garlic, peeled
2 tablespoons olive oil
1 teaspoon white wine vinegar
1½ cups yogurt
Salt
Pepper
4 to 6 cucumbers, peeled and diced

Mash garlic with olive oil. Add yogurt, season lightly with salt and pepper, and combine with diced cucumbers. Chill well before serving. Serve as a dip with crackers.

Makes about 2 cups.

CHICKEN TIKKA

2 broiling chickens (1½ to 2 pounds each), halved
4 cloves garlic, peeled
1 teaspoon salt
½ teaspoon ground ginger
½ teaspoon ground red pepper
2 teaspoons lemon juice
1 cup olive oil
Salt to taste

Wipe chicken dry and place in a shallow nonmetal bowl. Combine remaining ingredients; blend well. Put aside ½ cup of mixture and pour remaining mixture over chicken.

Marinate chicken 4 to 5 hours, turning frequently. Remove from marinade and wipe dry.

Broil over charcoal or under oven broiler. Baste frequently with marinade and sprinkle with additional salt. Heat reserved ½ cup of marinade and serve as sauce.

Serves 4.

BIRYANI

Meat and Sauce

4   tablespoons vegetable oil
1   pound beef round steak, cut into ¾-inch cubes
1   large onion, peeled and chopped
1   clove garlic, peeled and minced
1   1-inch piece fresh ginger, cut into cubes
½   cup yogurt
1   teaspoon salt
2   teaspoons ground cardamom
2   cloves
2   1-inch pieces of cinnamon stick
¼   teaspoon black pepper
2   cups water

Rice

6   cups water
1   teaspoon vegetable oil
2   cups long-grain rice
1   teaspoon ground cardamom
1   1-inch stick cinnamon
½   teaspoon saffron
½   cup milk

Heat 3 tablespoons of the vegetable oil in a large, deep stew pot. Add about ⅓ of the beef cubes and cook over medium heat until well browned on all sides. Remove meat with a slotted spoon and set aside. Repeat until all meat has been browned. Add fourth tablespoon of oil and onions to pot. Sauté until onions begin to take on a light golden color. Return meat to pot. Add garlic and ginger. Cook, stirring constantly, for 2 to 3 minutes. Remove pan from heat and stir in yogurt. Add remaining ingredients and blend well. Return pot to low heat. Cover partially and let simmer until meat is tender and liquid has been reduced to a thick sauce.

Prepare rice while meat cooks. In a large pot bring water to a full boil. Add oil, rice, cardamom and cinnamon. Bring water to a second boil, then reduce heat and let simmer for 15 minutes.

Drain rice into a large colander, then place in a large bowl. Combine saffron with milk. Blend and pour over rice. Place ½ of rice in a long, shallow baking dish. Spoon meat and sauce over surface and cover with remaining rice. Cover dish and place in a 325° F. oven. Bake 20 minutes. Mix and serve hot.

Serves 6.

CEDARS OF LEBANON

39 East 30th Street   *MU 6-9634*

Good Middle Eastern foods are served here on white tablecloths by Lebanese waiters. The style is "informal family" and the prices are low.

The restaurant is open every day from 11:45 A.M. to 10:00 P.M.

CARROT HALVAH

2	teaspoons butter
2	cups grated carrots
2	cups milk
1	teaspoon powdered cardamom
	Pinch of saffron
¼	cup sugar
¼	cup chopped almonds

Melt butter in a saucepan, add carrots and cook, stirring, over medium heat for 4 to 5 minutes. Add milk. Cover pan partially and let simmer until carrots are tender. Stir in remaining ingredients and continue to cook, stirring constantly, until mixture becomes thick and leaves the side of the pan. Serve hot or cold as an accompaniment to Beryami or curry dishes.

Serves 6.

DARDANELLES ARMENIAN RESTAURANT

86 University Place   *CH 2-8990*

Ask owner Melik Ohanesian for an Armenian recipe and, before he can answer, one of his relatives or waiters will tell you how Grandma made it in the old country.

The Dardanelles serves good Middle Eastern food with a special emphasis on Armenian specialties. The setting is pleasant and the people friendly. The lights are agreeably low and so is the Middle Eastern music.

The Dardanelles serves from noon to 9:30 P.M. On Saturday it is open from 1:00 P.M. to 11:00 P.M. and on Sunday from 1:00 P.M. to 9:00 P.M.

BREAD PUDDING

6	tablespoons butter
12	slices white bread
1	cup sugar
1	quart milk
1	teaspoon rose water
½	cup heavy cream
8	silver leaves
2	teaspoons slivered pistachio nuts
2	teaspoons slivered almonds

Melt the butter in a heavy skillet and pan-fry the bread slices until lightly browned. Place fried slices in a deep baking dish; sprinkle with sugar. Mix milk with rose water and pour over bread-sugar mixture. Bake in a slow oven for 45 minutes to 1 hour. Cool, cover with heavy cream, decorate with silver leaves and slivered nuts. Chill well before serving.

Serves 6.

SOUVLAKI

102 MacDougal Street
104 MacDougal Street
127 Chambers Street
825½ Broadway
21st Street at Fifth Avenue
113 Lafayette Street
117 East 15th Street

Souvlaki is a spit of ground meat. *Souvlaki* is also a sandwich made of this meat and an Arab pita bread. And Souvlaki is the name of seven luncheonette stands that serve *souvlaki, phallafel, hummus* and other savory Greek answers to Italian pizzas, the hero sandwich and Jewish delicatessen.

Coffee of all kinds can be gotten at Zabar's on upper Broadway, along with every kind of culinary equipment; breads, cheeses, fruits; and meats and fish of all descriptions—a kind of gourmet's paradise.

Aristedes Thanasoulis and Constantine Yfantopoulos are two young men from Greece who came to New York to study film making and started a little business on the side. Almost from the start, Souvlaki attracted mobs every lunch hour, and very soon the business grew. Aristedes and Constantine still hope to return to film making, but meanwhile they're busy serving fast-order Middle Eastern exotica at appetizingly low prices.

Souvlaki luncheonettes are open at varying hours.

SHISH KEBAB

3	pounds lean leg of lamb, cut into 1½-inch cubes
1	cup olive oil
¼	cup white vinegar
⅓	cup lemon juice
¼	cup red wine
4	whole cloves
1	bay leaf
1	teaspoon salt
½	teaspoon black pepper
1	tablespoon fresh dill weed
1	tablespoon chopped fresh parsley
4	green peppers, seeded and cut into 18 strips
18	small white onions
	Arabic bread

Place lamb in a large bowl; add oil, vinegar, lemon juice, wine, cloves, bay leaf, salt and pepper, dill weed and parsley. Blend so that each piece of meat is coated with spices. Cover and refrigerate 12 to 24 hours.

Parboil green pepper strips and onions in water to cover for 5 minutes. Drain and pat dry with paper toweling.

Spear meat onto 6 skewers alternately with green pepper strips and onions. Grill over charcoal fire or under oven broiler, basting with marinade and turning occasionally, for 15 to 20 minutes or until done to taste.

Heat Arabic bread and spread with drippings from meat. Place skewers on bread and serve at once.

Serves 6.

PART VI

Asian Food

Chapter XIV

INDIAN AND PAKISTANI FOOD

~~~~~~

Restaurants and Recipes

INDIA, the land of teas, poetry and Buddhism, has sent only a few thousand of her people to New York. And a number of these have come via Trinidad, British Guiana and the West Indies. Most of them are students, professors, businessmen and government personnel.

But for such a small representation of people, they have a sizable representation of restaurants in the city. The restaurants can be found on the Lower East Side, Upper West Side, in Harlem and midtown—everywhere, in fact, that the Indians and Pakistanis live and work, which is everywhere in the city.

The result of this volume of restaurants is that it is possible to find nearly every variety of curry in New York, ranging from one mild enough for the unaccustomed American palate to hot enough for the India-born Indian. Other Indian dishes are equally well represented.

INDIAN FOOD

The roots of Indian cuisine go back deep into history. In the year 4000 B.C. a tiny spot on the face of what is now Pakistan,

Playing the sitar in one of the many Indian restaurants in New York.

Mohenjo-Daro was a flourishing city, the center of a great civilization that even by our twentieth-century standards was highly developed. The well-to-do lived in comfortable brick houses; highly cultivated fields produced wheat, barley, peas, sesame, lemons and oranges. Herds of goats, sheep, cattle, pigs, chickens and ducks provided milk, butter, cheese, meat and eggs. Above all, they grew spices, mustard, saffron, fennel, cumin, tamarind and pepper.

These people were probably the first to cook vegetables and to season food in a deliberate attempt to improve its flavor. Spices were used to preserve foods as well. It was this subtle yet artful use of spices that led to curry, and while Indian food is far more than curry, nevertheless, spices do characterize the cuisine of the "monsoon countries" of India and Pakistan.

There are numerous excellent and authentic brands of curry powder on the market, but the true curry devotee blends his own mixture of coriander, cinnamon, cumin, turmeric and cardamom to suit the individual dish, which may in turn be made with almost any type of fish, meat, fowl or vegetable. In fact the word "curry" means a stew with more or less gravy depending on the richness of the dish.

Surprisingly enough, milk, at the opposite end of the culinary scale, is the other "common denominator" ingredient in Indian-Pakistani cooking. In the form of yogurt it makes the marinade for roast meats, smooths out the curry, and, mixed with chopped fresh vegetables, serves as an accompaniment. Sweet, it is used to make the universal *kheer,* a dessert pudding.

Indian food may seem adventurous. It is, but is an easy taste to acquire, and isn't adventure one of the pleasures of dining well?

RAJMAHAL RESTAURANT
124 Fourth Avenue   *473-9086*

Mossaddar Miah, a chef for 33 years, opened this Pakistani restaurant in 1967 and hired his family and friends to work with him. He makes his curries mild and then adds to them to suit each customer's taste. The restaurant does not aspire to great decor, just to excellent food, and on this point it succeeds.

Rajmahal is open from 11:30 A.M to 11:00 P.M. and on Friday and Saturday until midnight. On Sunday the hours are 4:00 P.M. to 10:30 P.M.

FIRNI
(Milk Custard with Almonds)

1½   quarts milk
1   cup sugar
½   cup raisins
2   tablespoons blanched and chopped almonds
1   tablespoon cornstarch
1   teaspoon rose water

Combine milk, sugar, raisins and almonds. Simmer slowly over low heat for about ½ hour. Remove from heat and add cornstarch; blend well. Return to heat and cook, stirring, until thick. Stir in rose water. Pour into serving bowl and chill well.

Serves 4 to 6.

SAMOSA
(With Minced Curry Filling)

½   cup vegetable shortening
2   cups flour
½   teaspoon salt
Ice water
Oil for frying
Minced curry filling (see below)

Lightly knead shortening into flour and salt. Add just enough ice water to make a soft dough. Divide into 8 balls and roll out each one on a lightly floured board to a circle about ⅛ inch thick. Place 2 tablespoons of filling on half of each circle and fold over. Cut across to make 2 triangle pastries; moisten edges and seal with a fork. Deep-fry in vegetable oil until crisp and lightly browned.

Pastries may be prepared and refrigerated or frozen (thaw before cooking) until ready to deep-fry. Serve hot with mint chutney.

Serves 4.

Minced Curry Filling

1	tablespoon butter
1	small onion (chopped)
½	pound ground beef
½	teaspoon ground ginger
¼	teaspoon garlic powder
¼	teaspoon red pepper
½	teaspoon salt
	Juice of ½ lemon

Heat butter in heavy skillet, add chopped onion, and sauté until limp but not brown. Add ground beef and all of the spices. Cook over medium heat until beef is well browned and very dry. Remove from heat and add lemon juice. Use to fill pastries as directed above.

MINT CHUTNEY

2	pounds fresh mint leaves
2	teaspoons tamarind juice
2	teaspoons unflavored yogurt
¼	teaspoon garlic powder
¼	teaspoon red pepper
¼	teaspoon salt

Crush mint leaves in a small bowl. Add remaining ingredients and mix well.

Serve with curries and kebabs.

About ¾ cup.

INDIA HOUSE EAST RESTAURANT

201 East 34th Street   *684-9367*

The chefs are two brothers from Bombay who cook in the Punjabi style of northern India. Their curries are authentically Indian with a mixture of spices and flavors only rarely found here. They do, however, use red pepper with a cautious hand.

India House serves lunch from 11:30 A.M. to 2:00 P.M. and

dinner from 5:00 P.M. to 11:30 P.M. No lunch is served on Saturday and Sunday.

VENDALOO

4   cloves garlic, peeled
¼   to ½ teaspoon chili powder
4   peppercorns
¼   teaspoon jerra seeds
½   teaspoon salt
2   tablespoons white wine vinegar
1   pound lean pork shoulder, cut into 1-inch cubes
2   to 3 tablespoons ghee or 1½ tablespoons butter
     and 1½ tablespoons vegetable oil
     Plain boiled rice

Place first 5 ingredients in electric blender and blend at low speed to a paste, or use a mortar and pestle and grind to a paste.

Place meat in a large nonmetal bowl. Add spice mixture, then turn and toss meat with a wooden spoon until each piece is coated with spices. Let stand 2 to 3 hours.

Heat ghee or butter and oil mixture in a large, heavy skillet (one with a heavy, tight-fitting cover). Add meat and stir over moderate heat until each piece is lightly browned. Cover skillet, reduce heat to low and let cook 30 to 45 minutes or until pork is tender. Spoon over plain boiled rice.

Serve with any desired sambals (curry condiment dishes), such as grated toasted coconut, currants, raisins, slivered almonds, mango chutney, etc.

Serves 4.

BIRYANI

2   tablespoons vegetable oil plus
     ¼ cup vegetable oil
3   large onions, peeled and sliced
4   whole cloves
8   cardamom seeds, peeled
2   cinnamon sticks
6   peppercorns
1   teaspoon ground cumin

1 teaspoon ground coriander
1 pound lean lamb, cut into 1- and 1½-inch cubes
½ pint yogurt
1 medium tomato, chopped
¼ cup water
Salt to taste
Plain boiled white rice
½ cup raisins
1 hard-cooked egg, chopped

Heat the 2 tablespoons oil in a small saucepan. Add the onion slices and sauté until deep golden in color. Remove from oil with a slotted spoon and place in electric blender; blend to a puree. Set aside.

Heat the ¼ cup oil in a large, heavy skillet and add the spices, whole cloves, cardamom seed and cinnamon sticks, the ground cumin and coriander. Cook, stirring, over moderate heat for 3 to 4 minutes. Increase heat, add lamb and cook, stirring often, until each piece is browned. Reduce heat to very low, pour in yogurt and stir to blend. Add chopped tomato, water and reserved onion puree. Cover skillet and let simmer until lamb is tender, about 1 hour. Season to taste with salt.

Spoon over just-cooked plain boiled rice and sprinkle a few raisins and chopped hard-cooked egg over each serving.

Serves 4.

GULAB JAMAN
(Raised Doughnuts)

4 cups pastry flour
½ teaspoon soda
2 cups yogurt
Oil for deep-frying
1 cup syrup (see recipe below)

Sift flour and soda together, combine with yogurt and knead together until well blended and the dough is smooth. Heat oil in deep, heavy fry kettle to 375° F. on deep-frying thermometer. Drop dough by spoonfuls into hot oil and fry, a few at a time, until they rise to the surface and are golden brown (1 or 2 minutes). Drain on paper toweling. Arrange in serving dishes

A quiet day in the old market near Atlantic Avenue, Brooklyn.

and pour warm syrup over each portion. Let soak 1 hour before serving.

Syrup

1½ cups sugar
1 cup water
½ teaspoon cloves
½ teaspoon cinnamon
Juice of 1 orange

Combine ingredients in saucepan and cook over medium heat until sugar dissolves and syrup thickens slightly. Cool before pouring over doughnuts.

KARACHI RESTAURANT

144 West 46th Street   *CI 5-9643*

Ahamad Meah came to this country and opened this second-floor restaurant 20 years ago "to cook real Indian food for an international clientele." The entrance to his restaurant is not very inviting and, once upstairs, the atmosphere is plain. But the prices are low, the service homey, and, most important, international curry fans love it. Mr. Meah, a Moslem, serves neither pork nor liquor.

Karachi is open from noon to 10:00 P.M. and on Friday and Saturday to 11:00 P.M. On Sunday the hours are 1:00 P.M. to 10:00 P.M.

PEA PULAO

2 cups uncooked long-grain rice
2 tablespoons salad oil
2 tablespoons butter
1 medium onion, peeled and thinly sliced
12 peppercorns
1 teaspoon ground cardamom
1 teaspoon whole cumin seed
1 ¼-inch piece of cinnamon stick
4 cups water
2 cups fresh uncooked green peas
¼ teaspoon salt

Soak rice in water for 1 to 2 hours. Heat salad oil and butter in heavy, deep saucepan. Add sliced onions and sauté until limp. Add spices and sauté for 5 minutes. Add water and bring to a boil; add rice and cook over medium heat until ½ of the water has been absorbed and rice is almost tender. Remove cinnamon stick; pour off all but about ¼ cup of remaining water. Add peas and salt. Cover tightly and cook over low heat until all water has been absorbed and rice is dry and fluffy and peas are tender (about 20 to 25 minutes).

Serves 6.

PARATHA

  1 cup whole wheat flour
  ½ teaspoon salt
  3 tablespoons butter (softened to room temperature)
     Water

Mix flour and salt. Knead 1 tablespoon of the soft butter into the flour-salt mixture; add enough water to make a soft dough. Knead well until smooth and velvety. Divide into 6 balls, flatten with fingers, dot with butter, and stack in layers of 3 with ¼ teaspoon of butter between each layer. Roll out each 3-layer "loaf" to ¼ inch thick and pan-fry one loaf at a time in the remaining butter until brown on both sides, turning only once. (Add more butter to pan if necessary.) Cut across and serve hot with curries and kebabs.

Serves 6.

MURGH CURRY

(Chicken Curry)

  ¼ cup salad oil
  ¼ cup butter
  1 2½-pound frying chicken (cut up for sauté)
  2 medium onions, peeled and thinly sliced
  1½ cups water
  2 teaspoons ground coriander
  ½ teaspoon garlic powder
  ½ teaspoon ginger

½   teaspoon red pepper
½   cup yogurt
1   teaspoon salt

Heat salad oil and butter in a large enamelized cast-iron sauté pan. Dry chicken pieces with paper toweling and sauté over medium heat in oil-butter mixture until lightly browned. Remove chicken to hot platter and keep warm. Sauté onions in fat over low heat until limp but not brown. Add water and all of the spices. Cook, stirring, for 5 to 10 minutes. Return chicken to pan; add yogurt and salt. Stir to blend. Cover and simmer over low heat for 25 to 30 minutes or until chicken is tender and sauce has thickened. Serve hot over cooked rice.
Serves 6.

FIRNI

(Milk Custard with Rice)

1   cup uncooked rice
1   quart milk
1   cup sugar
1   cup slivered pistachio nuts
¼   cup silver cake dusting (optional)

Soak rice in cold water for 1 to 2 hours. Heat milk in non-metal saucepan to near boiling point, add rice, reduce heat to low and simmer slowly until mixture begins to thicken; add sugar and mix well. Continue to cook for 5 minutes. Cool and pour into serving dish. Decorate top with pistachio nuts and silver cake dusting. Chill thoroughly before serving.
Serves 4 to 6.

CHICKEN FAROOQ

2   medium onions, peeled and chopped fine
4   cloves garlic, peeled and crushed
½   teaspoon ground red pepper
1   teaspoon salt
1   cup yogurt
1   1½-pound broiler chicken (cut up for sauté)
4   tablespoons vegetable oil

Mix onion, garlic, red pepper, salt and yogurt in a glass or earthenware bowl. Place chicken pieces in mixture, cover and marinate in the refrigerator for 4 to 5 hours, turning occasionally.

Drain chicken and pat dry, reserving marinade. Heat oil in heavy enamelized iron sauté pan, add chicken and cook over medium heat until lightly browned. Pour off accumulated fat and cover with marinade. Continue to cook, covered, for 20 to 25 minutes, or until chicken is tender and sauce has thickened. Serve over hot rice.

Serves 4 to 6.

Worshippers entering Christian Science Church on MacDougal Street, Greenwich Village.

Chapter XV

CHINESE FOOD

~~~~~~

Restaurants and Recipes

OF ALL THE foreign "cities" within New York City, no other
is so strong and so tightly knit as Chinatown. It is conceivable for
a child to have been born in Chinatown, New York, in 1940 or
1950 and to have grown up with as strong a Chinese accent and
as strong a Chinese life-style as his uncle who came over from
Canton in 1920.

Ninety years ago, when the Chinese first appeared in New
York in numbers, they began to settle within the invisible walls
of a triangle bordered by Canal Street, Mulberry Street and
Broadway. Today there are about 55,000 of them and the bor-
ders have begun to expand across Broadway into other parts
of the Lower East Side.

Chinatown is always lively and bustling, vibrating and throb-
bing, from early morning when the community awakes until
early the next morning when those restaurants with all-night
business close at 5:00 A.M.

But no day is like Sunday in Chinatown. Then thousands
and thousands come—the Chinese from as far as New Jersey,
Pennsylvania and Connecticut, to buy ginger root, duck eggs,
dried shrimp, seaweed, soybean curd and lotus seeds; the

Americans to eat in the seemingly endless little restaurants that are stacked against, under and above each other like so many precariously placed cards; and tourists to stare at the concentration of people and businesses, at telephone booths shaped like miniature pagodas and at the incredible juxtaposition of Chinese characters and Chinese sounds against New Yorkese, Spanish, Jewish, Italian, German, Swedish and every other language spoken by the strollers—if people crawling at a mob's pace can be called strollers—on a sunny Sunday afternoon in Chinatown.

The Chinese Restaurant Association says there are 2,000 Chinese restaurants in the metropolitan area, with the greatest number in Manhattan. More than 90 percent of them feature the Cantonese style of cooking, but recently there have been a spate of restaurants featuring Northern or Mandarin and Szechuan food styles.

There is no section of town now that does not have a Chinese restaurant, and, in fact, there is at least one new one opening every few weeks. But the heaviest concentration is still in Chinatown and by far so are the best bargains and the best sights.

CHINESE COOKING

The best-known method of Chinese cooking in this country, *ch'ao*—which translates roughly to "low-oil-quick-stir-frying"—contributes much to an understanding of this highly sophisticated and ancient cuisine. In *ch'ao* cookery meat or seafood (or both) and vegetables are cut into uniformly small pieces, then quickly stir-fried in a small quantity of oil over very high heat. An infinitesimal amount of liquid is added and in a moment the dish is done to perfection. It sounds simple, and of course it is, but in the hands of a knowledgeable Chinese chef, *ch'ao* cooking is transformed into both a delicate science and a skillful art. Each ingredient is added at precisely the right moment so that all are cooked to the same degree of doneness, none is overcooked, no nutrients are lost and all natural flavor is

A wall of beautiful Chinese pin-ups adorning the grocery's storeroom in Chinatown. Note the ever-present abacus lying atop the boxes of packaged Chinese delicacies.

Utensils hanging on the wall at the entrance to a Chinese grocery store in New York's Chinatown. Note the abacus on the counter.

retained. These qualities are the essence of all Chinese food, the prevailing theme that unites many provincial styles of cooking, each different, but each uniquely Chinese.

The Chinese gourmet, like the French gourmet, starts the meal at the market. Finding the finest vegetables, the freshest fish or the best-quality meat determines the menu. The next step is choosing the best method of cooking the food and in what combinations.

Most Chinese dishes are a mixture of many ingredients. Lobster, chicken, and shrimp, pork and seafood or chicken and ham are combined and stir-fried, or steamed with appropriate vegetables; bamboo shoots, snow peas, cabbage, onions and such are teamed with dried or fresh mushrooms, water chestnuts, fresh ginger root, soy sauce and numerous other spices.

The Chinese cook rarely uses more than one or two tablespoons of water in any dish. To boil food, then discard the water is to throw away the nutrition as well as the flavor. Instead, steam is the cooking agent. Called *jing*, steam cooking is used in the Chinese kitchen with great effect. A whole fish placed on a heatproof platter is brushed with oil, soy sauce and Chinese rice wine, sprinkled with diced ginger and scallions, placed over boiling water and steamed until cooked *au point*, deliciously done with full flavor intact. Lobsters, clams and crabs are cooked in the same whirling sea of steam, and so are meats, as well as a very Chinese, un-Western, salty, nonsweet custard. Made with eggs and water combined with bite-size chunks of shrimp or other seafood, flavored with soy sauce and scallions, it is a beautiful dish, colorful, fragrant and immensely appetizing.

Though Chinese food is high on the list of the world's great cuisines, it is nonetheless more often simple than elaborate. Though roasted, deep-fried and grilled foods are served on special occasions, the preferred everyday methods of cooking are *ch'ao* (stir-fried) and *jing* (steamed) (which just may be the reason that the average Chinese looks younger than his years, is very seldom overweight and rarely has high blood pressure or heart disease). It does not follow, however, that Chinese cooking is bland; far from it, in fact. It is the delicate and subtle, yet decided seasoning of Chinese food that gives this cuisine such universal appeal. Dried mushrooms add woodsy flavor, not unlike fresh truffles. Spicy ginger root and "Five Spice Powder," a blend of ground cloves, Chinese star anise, cinnamon, fennel and licorice root, make any dish festive fare. Soy sauces, sweet Hoisin sauces and oyster sauce are used in judicious combinations. The special blandness of bean curd points up the just-from-the-garden crispness of vegetables, and aromatic sesame oil, Chinese rice wine, red bean paste and sesame seeds are teamed with such less exotic seasonings as sugar, vinegar and salt to produce a range of flavor unheard of and untasted until China opened its doors to the Western world.

THE MANDARIN HOUSE

133 West 13th Street   *WA 9-0551*

The plan of this pleasant Northern Chinese restaurant includes a pebble-floored courtyard used year round—open in summer, enclosed and heated in winter. In addition there is a large dining room with pleasantly spaced tables for maximum privacy.

The Mandarin House is open from noon to midnight and to 1:00 A.M. on Friday and Saturday.

SHREDDED SPICED BEEF

  1   pound flank steak, shredded*

    Marinade:
      1   egg white, unbeaten
      1   tablespoon dry sherry
      1   tablespoon water
      1   tablespoon sesame oil
      1   tablespoon cornstarch

  3   cups vegetable oil for deep-frying
  3   tablespoons sesame oil for stir-frying

* Freeze beef overnight; it will be easier to slice and shred.

1 cup (canned) bamboo shoots, shredded and well drained
1 large carrot, scraped and shredded
2 ribs celery, shredded
1 clove garlic, peeled and minced
1 small cube fresh ginger, finely chopped
1½ teaspoons hot pepper oil
3 tablespoons soy sauce
1 tablespoon white wine vinegar
1½ teaspoons sugar
¼ teaspoon monosodium glutamate
1 teaspoon sesame seed oil
Chinese fried noodles

Combine shredded beef with egg white, sherry, water, sesame oil and cornstarch. Let stand 30 minutes.

Place the 3 cups of oil in a deep, heavy frying kettle and heat to 375° F. on a deep-frying thermometer. Place meat in deep-fat fry basket, lower into hot oil and fry for 2 minutes. Add shredded bamboo shoots, carrots and celery; deep-fry 1 minute. Remove from oil and drain thoroughly on paper toweling. Set aside.

Heat 2 tablespoons of the sesame oil in a Chinese wok or a deep, heavy sauté pan. Add garlic and ginger and stir-fry for 1 or 2 seconds over medium heat. Stir in soy sauce, vinegar, sugar, hot pepper oil and monosodium glutamate. Blend quickly, then add deep-fried beef, bamboo shoots, carrots and celery, and remaining 1 tablespoon sesame oil, and stir for 1 minute. Transfer to serving dish, garnish with fried noodles and serve at once.

FISH WITH BEAN CURD

1 whole sea bass, scaled and cleaned
½ teaspoon salt
1 tablespoon dry sherry
4 tablespoons vegetable oil
1 clove garlic, peeled and minced
2½ tablespoons soy sauce
2 tablespoons sugar
4 2-inch slices fresh ginger
½ cup water

Three generations of a Chinese-American family at lunch in a

Chinatown noodle shop.

½	cup bamboo shoots (canned)
2	pieces dried mushrooms (soak in boiling water for 30 minutes; discard stems)
¼	teaspoon monosodium glutamate
1	3-inch piece fresh bean curd cut into 6 slices
1½	teaspoons cornstarch dissolved in 3 tablespoons water
2	scallions (white part only), shredded

Rub fish with salt, sprinkle with sherry, let stand 10 minutes. Wipe dry with paper towel. Heat oil in deep, heavy sauté pan. Fry fish for 3 minutes on each side over low heat. Add garlic, soy sauce, sugar, ginger, water, bamboo shoots, mushrooms and monosodium glutamate. Cover pan and cook over medium heat for 6 minutes. Add bean curd and cook for another 6 minutes. Gradually add the dissolved cornstarch and stir gently until sauce has thickened. Place fish and sauce on large platter, sprinkle fish with sesame oil and garnish with shredded scallions. Serve very hot.

Serves 4.

HO HO RESTAURANT

131 West 50th Street *CI 6-3256*

"We were one of the first restaurants in New York to offer Northern cuisine—and that was 20 years ago," says George Seto, manager and part owner of this sumptuously styled Chinese restaurant. Their present menu lists both Northern and Cantonese dishes. While the menu is not especially long, many of the choices are impressively out of the ordinary.

The restaurant's present styling is modern Oriental, with a ferocious dragon wrapped around a floor-to-ceiling pole and a pleasant Oriental garden to greet you at the entrance, and the tinkle of an indoor fountain to soothe you in the rear of the main dining room.

Ho Ho is open from 11:30 A.M. to 3:00 A.M. On Sunday it opens at 12:30 P.M.

This great golden god sits in a window in New York's Chinatown, receiving coins from visitors in exchange for good wishes.

CHIN CHIAO

(Shredded Beef)

2	dried Chinese black mushrooms
1	pound center-cut flank steak
1	teaspoon sugar
1	teaspoon salt
1	tablespoon dry sherry
4	tablespoons soy sauce
1	large green pepper
1	rib celery
½	cup bamboo shoots
2	tablespoons vegetable oil
1	teaspoon cornstarch

Soak mushrooms in cold water to cover for 2 hours. Drain, pat dry and cut crosswise into shreds, i.e., matchlike pieces.

Shred the flank steak, i.e., cut across the grain into matchlike pieces. Combine sugar, salt, sherry and 2 tablespoons of the soy sauce. Pour over meat and let stand 10 minutes.

Cut green pepper lengthwise in half, discard seeds and shred halves as above. Shred celery in like manner. Combine shredded green pepper, celery, mushrooms and bamboo shoots.

Heat oil in wok or heavy skillet. Drain meat and add, cooking over high heat until barely brown. Add mixed vegetables and stir-fry until peppers are tender.

Mix cornstarch with remaining soy sauce. Stir into meat mixture. Stir to blend and cook, stirring, until meat and vegetables are glazed with sauce. Serve immediately with dry white rice.

Serves 4.

LAM KEE RESTAURANT

3 Catherine Street   *CA 6-9572*

The front of this tiny neighborhood Shanghai-style restaurant in Chinatown is so dim you're likely to miss it. If you do discover it, you'll find the inside a bright, steamy place with at least four of its five closely packed tables filled with chatting Chinese.

English is virtually unknown here, and you'll order by writing down the numbers of the dishes you want from the Chinese character–approximate English menu. Pad and pencil are always provided for ordering, but napkins are often forgotten and getting a glass of water is a struggle.

The benefits—and surely there must be benefits—are surprisingly good food, very low prices and an uncommon, untouristy view of Chinatown.

Lam Kee is open from 11:30 A.M. to 10:00 P.M. Closed Monday.

PAI KWOH

(Chinese Spareribs)

2	pounds spareribs
1	garlic clove, minced
1	cup honey
2	tablespoons sesame oil
1	1-inch cube ginger, chopped
¼	cup soy sauce
¼	cup sake (rice wine)
1	teaspoon salt

Cut ribs into serving portions. Combine remaining ingredients in large nonmetal bowl. Marinate ribs in mixture for at least three hours in refrigerator. Drain, pat dry. Place in shallow baking dish and bake in preheated 350° F. oven for 1½ hours, basting frequently with remaining marinade until crisp and well done.

Serves 4.

PAGODA

41 Mott Street   *WO 2-5650*

The menu at Pagoda is as impressively long as the restaurant is impressively old. This upstairs Cantonese dining room has been an integral part of Chinatown for more than 60 years, and it has a large number of faithful followers—both Chinese

Chinese New Year's Day parade, Mott Street, Chinatown.

and American. Attention to design starts and stops with the presentation of the food; there is evidently none left over for decor.

The Pagoda is open from 11:00 A.M. to 11:30 P.M. and on Saturday until 2:30 A.M.

CRYSTAL SHRIMPS

2	pounds raw shrimp
4	tablespoons salt
3	tablespoons peanut oil
¼	clove garlic, minced
1	tablespoon finely chopped fresh ginger
1	tablespoon dry white wine
1	medium tomato, peeled, seeded and diced
2	tablespoons soy sauce
½	teaspoon pepper
½	teaspoon salt
1	teaspoon sugar
½	teaspoon cornstarch
2	scallions, finely minced

Shell and devein shrimp. Rub well with salt, then wash with running water. Place shrimp in glass or earthenware bowl under barely running water and allow to stand for at least 30 minutes. Drain and pat dry. Heat oil in deep, heavy enamelized cast-iron sauté pan, add garlic and ginger, and cook, stirring, over medium heat 2 to 3 minutes; add shrimp and stir briefly; add wine and tomatoes and cook for 2 minutes longer; add remaining ingredients and cook for a final 2 or 3 minutes. Serve hot over rice.

NOTE: It is important that cooking time does not exceed 5 or 6 minutes.

Serves 6.

SZECHUAN VILLAGE

1 University Place   *673-3801*

There is a small but growing number of Chinese restaurants in New York that claim allegiance to the spicy cooking style of

Szechuan, a south-central province of China. Szechuan Village is one of the more attractive of these restaurants. It has a large, cool, dimly lit dining room with murals of traditional scenes of China. The service is pleasant even if there sometimes is a bit of a language problem.

Szechuan Village is open every day from 11:00 A.M. to midnight.

SLICED PRAWNS WITH GARLIC SAUCE

3   pounds raw shrimp
    Peanut or sesame oil for deep-frying
2   egg whites, lightly beaten
½   cup hot pepper oil*
1   clove garlic, minced
1   tablespoon chopped fresh ginger
6   water chestnuts, thinly sliced
1   "wooden ear,"** chopped

Peel and devein shrimp; cut into thirds. Heat oil in deep, heavy fry kettle. Dip shrimp pieces in beaten egg white. Fry in deep hot oil for a few seconds until just golden brown. Drain on paper toweling and keep hot.

Heat the hot pepper oil in a sauté pan, add garlic and cook over low heat until transparent. Add ginger, water chestnuts and "wooden ear." Cook briefly to blend, add shrimp and sauté over high heat for 3 to 4 minutes. Serve over hot cooked rice. Serves 6.

SZECHUAN SHRIMP

2   pounds raw shrimp
2   egg whites
2   tablespoons cornstarch
¾   cup finely chopped green onions
½   cup finely chopped bamboo shoots
½   cup chopped hot green pepper
1   tablespoon grated fresh ginger
2   tablespoons chopped shallots
1½ tablespoons finely chopped garlic

* Hot pepper oil is available in Chinese food stores.
** A "wooden ear" is a fungus similar to a truffle and also available in Chinese food stores.

1 cup finely chopped ripe tomatoes with juice
1 tablespoon soy sauce
2 tablespoons sherry
2 tablespoons hot pepper oil
½ teaspoon monosodium glutamate
1 teaspoon cornstarch
2 tablespoons Hoisin sauce
2 cups plus 2 tablespoons peanut oil
Boiled rice

Shell and devein shrimp. Wash under cold water and pat dry. Beat egg whites to a light froth and beat in cornstarch. When well blended, add the shrimp and stir to coat well. Marinate shrimp in egg-white mixture for 5 hours in refrigerator. Blend green onions, bamboo shoots, hot green pepper, fresh ginger, shallots and garlic; set aside.

Combine tomatoes, soy sauce, sherry, hot pepper oil and monosodium glutamate in small saucepan. Cook briefly until tomatoes are liquid. Mix cornstarch with Hoisin sauce until smooth, add to tomato mixture and cook only until slightly thickened. Set aside.

Fill a deep saucepan with 2 cups of the peanut oil. Heat to medium; the fat must not be too hot. Place the marinated shrimp in a sieve or deep-fry basket and cook for 1 minute in the hot oil; do not brown.

Heat the remaining 2 tablespoons of oil in a Chinese wok or heavy sauté pan, add the shrimp and the green onion–bamboo shoot mixture, and cook quickly for 1 or 2 minutes, stirring constantly. Add the tomato mixture and cook quickly until the shrimps are well coated and piping hot. Serve at once over hot boiled rice.

Serves 6.

LOTUS EATERS ROYALE

59 East 56th Street   *HA 1-5580*

The Chinese consider color, flavor, texture, taste and design in preparing their food. The same salient points were evidently considered in preparing the dining rooms of this sophisticated Chinese restaurant. The effect is handsome Chinese-modern. The dishes served here are excellent examples of Shanghai and Szechuan cooking.

Lotus Eaters Royale is open every day from 11:30 A.M. to 11:00 P.M.

CHINESE FRIED CHICKEN

1   1½- to 2-pound chicken, boned
1   cup flour
1   teaspoon baking powder
½   teaspoon salt
2   eggs
¼   cup milk
    Peanut or sesame oil for frying

Have butcher bone chicken. Cut into 1½-inch cubes. Sift together flour, baking powder and salt. Beat eggs with milk and add to flour mixture. Blend well. Let stand for 15 minutes. Heat oil to 375° F. on deep-frying thermometer in deep, heavy skillet. Dip chicken pieces in batter and fry (a few pieces at a time) until golden brown.

Serves 4 to 6.

SZECHUAN BEEF

(Hot Spiced Shredded Beef)

1   pound beef sirloin, shredded
2   tablespoons peanut oil
2   tablespoons bamboo shoots, shredded
1   carrot, shredded
3   tablespoons dried hot pepper
¼   cup soy sauce
1   teaspoon sugar
¼   teaspoon salt

Have butcher cut meat with the grain—this is very important; otherwise meat will fall apart during cooking. Heat oil in heavy skillet; add beef, bamboo shoots, carrots and peppers. Cook briefly over high heat until meat is no longer red (about 3 minutes). Add soy sauce, sugar and salt, and cook 1 minute longer, just until thoroughly hot. Serve over cooked rice.

Serves 4.

Chapter XVI

KOREAN FOOD

〜〜〜〜〜〜〜〜〜〜〜〜〜〜〜〜〜〜〜〜〜〜〜〜〜〜〜〜〜〜〜

Restaurants and Recipes

NEW YORK's Korean population is still very small and composed mostly of students, diplomats and other government personnel who tend to stay together in the Morningside Heights area of the Upper West Side.

Despite its tumultuous history as a battleground for stronger Asian nations, Korea managed to emerge after World War II with its own clearly indigenous culture intact.

And nowhere in New York is this cultural distinction more evident than in the cuisine found at the growing number of Korean restaurants. The Chinese and Japanese influences are there, certainly, but they do not mask the fact that Korean food is a thing apart.

Most of the Korean restaurants are on the West Side, but a few, notably the New Korea, are gaining a sizable following on the East Side.

NEW KOREA

9 East 40th Street   *MU 3-7775*

This new Korean restaurant in midtown Manhattan was a success almost from its beginning two years ago. And for a num-

A Chinese vegetable store in Chinatown.

ber of good reasons. The restaurant has two large, nicely decorated dining rooms that are a pleasure to dine in. The food is of a special and exotic quality. The prices are sensible. And there is tender and courteous service by *tschima chokori*–clad waitresses.

New Korea is open every day, serving lunch from noon to 3:00 P.M. and dinner from 5:00 P.M. to 11:00 P.M.

BUL GO KI
(Sirloin Slices Marinated and Broiled)

2	pounds top sirloin
1	cup sesame oil
½	cup soy sauce
1	tablespoon sesame seeds
1	teaspoon black pepper
1	clove garlic, minced

Have the butcher cut the sirloin in extra-thin slices. Combine remaining ingredients in nonmetal bowl and marinate meat in mixture for at least 3 hours. Broil quickly, preferably over charcoal, turning only once.

Serves 6.

OHI NA MOOL
(Marinated Cucumbers)

4	medium cucumbers
½	cup soy sauce
¼	cup vinegar
¼	cup sesame oil
2	teaspoons dried hot peppers*
1	teaspoon sugar
1	tablespoon rice powder*
½	teaspoon salt
1	teaspoon soy bean powder*
¼	cup water

Peel and slice cucumbers as thinly as possible. Combine remaining ingredients in a glass or earthenware bowl (not metal).

* Available in Japanese food stores.

Blend well, add cucumbers and marinate in the refrigerator for at least 1 hour. Serve cold.

Serves 4.

KIMCHEE
(Pickled Chinese Cabbage)

Served with almost all Korean meals.

1 large head Chinese cabbage
3 tablespoons salt
1 clove garlic, minced
1 tablespoon ground hot red peppers
3 scallions, minced
1 tablespoon chopped fresh ginger
1 tablespoon sugar
2 tablespoons *sae woo juk**
2 medium turnips, peeled and thinly sliced

Wash cabbage well, cut in quarters and soak in cold water with the salt for at least 8 hours or overnight. Drain and wash again; chop coarsely. Mix remaining ingredients in a glass or earthenware or other nonmetal bowl. Add chopped cabbage, mix well, cover and refrigerate for 1 or 2 days.** Serve cold.

Serves 4.

ARIRANG KOREAN RESTAURANT

30 West 56th Street   *LT 1-9698*

The food in this eight-year-old Korean restaurant is interesting and unusual, the setting is handsome and understated and the atmosphere is serene as waitresses wearing their native *tschima chokori* dress pad about on thickly carpeted floors.

Arirang House serves lunch from noon to 2:30 P.M. and dinner from 5:00 P.M. to 10:30 P.M. Closed Sunday.

* The *sae woo juk* may be omitted if desired, but it adds an authentic touch. This ingredient may be purchased at Japanese food stores.

** The Koreans marinate the cabbage for 5 to 6 days, but Occidentals will probably find the shorter marination more to their taste.

Barbecued ducks hanging ready, waiting to be bought, in one of

Chinatown's many grocery and delicacy shops.

DUENJANG KUK

(Beef and Bean Curd Soup)

6 cups clear beef stock or broth
½ cup top round of beef cut into slivers
1 large scallion, finely chopped
¼ small white turnip, peeled and minced
3 cakes bean curd, cut into ½-inch cubes
3 large scallops, finely chopped
3 tablespoons soy sauce

Combine all ingredients in saucepan and bring to boil. Lower heat and let simmer for 15 to 20 minutes. Serve very hot in small bowls.

Serves 8.

Chapter XVII

JAPANESE FOOD

≈≈≈≈≈≈≈≈≈≈≈≈≈≈≈≈≈≈≈≈≈≈≈≈≈≈≈≈≈≈

Restaurants and Recipes

JUST BEFORE World War I, the first Japanese eating place in New York was established on the West Side. It was the dining room of a boardinghouse, and it catered to the city's tiny Japanese population who longed for the foods of their homeland.

Eventually other Japanese restaurants opened, but it took two world wars and an international treaty before a large influx of Japanese brought the recent spate of new Japanese restaurants to New York.

Since the United States signed the Treaty of Friendship, Commerce and Navigation with Japan in the 1950s, more businessmen, bankers, students, professors and diplomats from that country have come to New York than ever before. The city now has about 8,000 Japanese, more than 300 offices of Japanese companies and the Bank of Tokyo.

With them the Japanese have brought their highly refined and polished culture—*haiku* (17-syllable poetry), *ikebana* (flower arrangement), and of course their carefully timed, artistically arranged foods and exquisitely executed restaurants.

Eleven years ago there were no more than ten Japanese res-

The photographer said, "Smile," at Rockefeller Center on a pretty summer day.

taurants in New York. Today there are nearly 80, and new ones continue to open every few weeks.

Many of these restaurants are traditional in design, bringing the serene aura of old Japan to New York. Others are as sleek as a modern Tokyo establishment. Still others would be outwardly indistinguishable from any of the city's thousands of luncheonettes were it not for an occasional Japanese sign, the language problem, and the lingering aroma of *shogu, sushi* and *sukiyaki*.

While the Japanese live in many areas of the city, the area of Broadway and 110th Street is considered the principal Japanese neighborhood. Accordingly, a number of small Japanese restaurants have opened nearby. Other Japanese restaurants, from the modern and sleek to the luncheonette variety, can now be found in most areas of the city.

But the most beautiful Japanese inns, those which have been designed in Japan and built here by Japanese and are like elegant Oriental temples of serenity and impeccable quiet taste, are to be found in mid-Manhattan, both east and west of Fifth Avenue. They represent the truest touch of the Orient in New York.

JAPANESE FOOD

The art of slowly cooking a melange of ingredients in one pot so that flavors blend and merge together for a succulent stew or casserole is virtually unknown in Japan. Instead, Japanese cooks seek a totally different result. What they aim for is to bring out the flavor of each component of the dish so that each contrasts and complements the others in taste and texture.

Cutting and preparing the raw ingredients is a precise art in Japanese kitchens. Great attention is given to color and texture contrasts; to the Japanese gourmet the way that food is presented is equally as important as the way it tastes.

Though cooking time is short by comparison to a European or even an American "hurry-up" meal, each morsel of vegetable, seafood or meat is exactly timed for perfection. Green vegetables are served still beautifully green and fish retains a taste of the sea, while carrots, eggplant, onions and such remain crisp but nonetheless tender.

Japanese main-course dishes are, in general, sweeter than Occidental ones. Sugar is used in almost every dish both as a seasoning and as a catalyst to help bring out subtle taste elements. The one seasoning of primary importance to the authenticity of Japanese food is *aji-no-moto*—monosodium glutamate, often called "taste power" in Japan as it intensifies and brings up the natural flavor of any food on which it is used. Other essential seasonings are *shogu,* Japanese soy sauce, and *mirin,* a thick, sweet rice wine.

Rice is the basic element of all Japanese meals. It is bread and potatoes to the Japanese and it is served with the simplest as well as with the most elaborate meals. Though Japanese cooks prepare rice in a number of different ways and with a variety of ingredients, plain steamed white rice is the national favorite. Against this bland taste other flavors are greatly accentuated as color against a neutral background.

No mention of Japanese cuisine can ignore tea. It is not only the national beverage but a way of life to every man, woman and child in Japan. Tea begins the day and the meal, tea is the start as well as the finish. Believed to be beneficial to the spirit as well as the body, tea and the Japanese tea ceremony perhaps best express the Japanese attitude toward food. Formal and ritualistic, exquisite to see as well as to eat and drink, it epitomizes the ultimate in Japanese cuisine, food that is a delight to the eye as well as the taste.

KEGON JAPANESE RESTAURANT
80 East 56th Street   *421-8777*

Kegon says that the taste of Japanese food is dependent on the surrounding atmosphere. And the surrounding atmosphere at Kegon is certainly conducive to good taste. As if its serene, traditional decor were not enough, Kegon has imported two geishas to lend their beauty and talents to this handsome restaurant.

Cooking sukiyaki at the table in the Japanese manner at Benihana East.
The girls who serve all wear the traditional Japanese costume.

Mother Nature & Sons, an organic food store on Bleecker Street in the West Village. This mushroomed from the owner, Abbe Borov's, desire to find the kind of food he wanted himself. Now others like him beat a path to his door.

Kegon serves lunch from noon to 3:00 P.M. and dinner from 5:30 P.M. to 1:00 A.M. There is no lunch served on Saturday. Closed Sunday.

MIZUTAKI

1   3-pound chicken
    Chicken stock or water to cover
    Salt
6   scallions, cut into 1-inch lengths
1   medium-sized onion, peeled and sliced thin
1   bunch watercress, trimmed
1   cup lemon juice
1   cup soy sauce
1   cup Japanese wine (sake)
1   level teaspoon monosodium glutamate
      (*aji-no-moto* or Ac'cent)

Have the butcher divide the chicken in half and cut or chop it into 1½-inch cubes without bones. Place the pieces in a heavy saucepan and cover with chicken stock or water. Add a little salt and simmer gently for 45 minutes after the boiling point is reached.

Bring to the table in an electric skillet or in the cooking utensil and place over a charcoal or alcohol burner so that the liquid barely boils. When guests are seated, commence adding vegetables to the simmering broth, a few at a time. To serve, spoon a few portions of the meat and barely cooked vegetables into small serving bowls. Using chopsticks or forks, guests dip bite-sized bits of chicken into a sauce made by combining lemon juice, soy sauce, sake and monosodium glutamate.

NOTE: *Mizutaki* should be served with hot cooked rice.

Serves 2 to 4.

SUSHI DISHES

Pack *sushi* rice into small individual round custard cups. Let stand 30 minutes or until firm. Then run a small knife around edges of cups so that you can remove the rice without breaking it. Place each rice mold in a small, attractive lacquered bowl. Top with paper-thin slices of very fresh tuna, red snapper or striped bass. Place a dot of green mustard on each slice of fish. Serve with a second small bowl of *shoyu* (soy) sauce for dunking.

Place 1 piece of *norimaki* (seaweed) on a wooden chopping board. Cover with a thin layer of *sushi* rice. Over this, place a paper-thin slice of raw red snapper. Place a long, thin strip of pickle crosswise in the center. Starting at one long end, roll up jelly-roll fashion, pressing firmly together as you roll. Trim off uneven ends of roll and cut into 1-inch sections. Arrange sections on serving plates, cut side up, so that filling is visible.

Soak 4 to 6 dried forest mushrooms in warm water and cover for about 15 minutes. Drain and discard stalks. Place in a small saucepan. Cover with fresh water and let simmer until tender. Add 1 pound sugar and continue to cook 3 or 4 minutes. Then add 1 tablespoon *shoyu* sauce and cook until mushrooms have absorbed all liquid. Remove from heat and cut into narrow strips.

Fill well-scrubbed clam shells with *sushi* rice and top each with strips of prepared mushrooms. Garnish each with a little red caviar.

Rice for Sushi Dishes

1	cup rice
1½	cups water
1	4-inch piece of kelp
½	cup vinegar
2	tablespoons sugar
1	teaspoon salt
¼	teaspoon monosodium glutamate

Wash rice thoroughly by running it through several changes of water. Drain in colander and let stand 45 minutes to 1 hour before cooking.

Place rice and water in saucepan. Float kelp on water. Place over high heat, cover and bring to a full boil. Reduce heat to medium. Remove kelp and quickly re-cover pot. Let cook for 10 minutes, then further reduce heat to very low and let rice steam for 10 minutes. Remove pot from heat and let stand covered for 10 minutes.

In a small saucepan heat vinegar with sugar, salt and monosodium glutamate. Transfer rice to a large, shallow wooden salad bowl. With an old-fashioned Japanese (or other) fan, cool the rice by fanning it with one hand while you pour the vinegar mixture into it. Then quickly, with a wooden spoon, lift and fold until mixture is evenly distributed through rice and it is dry.

NOTE: Keep rice covered during entire cooking process except when quickly removing kelp. At no time during cooking should rice be stirred. For best results, use imported Japanese rice.

SAITO RESTAURANT

131 West 52nd Street   *JU 2-7809*

One of the first fine Japanese restaurants in New York, Saito is also one of the most dignified and beautiful. The decor, the design, the tableware are all from Japan. The food is prepared to the exacting standards of Japanese cuisine, and the service is in the Japanese tradition of courtesy and grace.

Saito introduced the first *age*-bar, or tempura bar, in the United States, where it serves at least a half-dozen varieties of golden, deep-fried seafood.

Saito serves lunch from noon to 3:00 P.M. and dinner from 5:30 P.M. to 10:30 P.M. Closed Sunday.

BEEF SUKIYAKI

Sukiyaki is basically a combination of sliced meat and vegetables cooked in a savory *shoyu* sauce, fast to fix and fun to cook, the guests transferring morsels of food directly from the saucepan to their bowls while the *sukiyaki* is still cooking.

Arrange the following ingredients on a large serving platter and bring to the table:

3	ounces beef suet
1½	pounds tenderloin of beef, sliced very thin
12	scallions cut into 2-inch lengths
1	Bermuda onion, sliced into ¼-inch thickness
1	bunch watercress
2	cups *shirataki* (vermicelli)

4   large mushrooms, sliced
1   *tofu* (fresh bean curd), cut into 1-inch cubes
1   small can bamboo shoots, cut into thin lengthwise strips

Sauce

1   cup beef consommé
½   cup *shoyu**
½   cup *mirin* (Japanese cooking wine)**
1   heaping teaspoon sugar**
½   teaspoon monosodium glutamate

To prepare sauce, mix all ingredients. Pour into small pitcher and set aside.

Cut suet into small pieces and place in hot saucepan. When sufficient fat is melted, add enough sauce to cover bottom of saucepan. Add the sliced Bermuda onions and scallions and cook 1–2 minutes. Add the remaining sauce, *shirataki,* mushrooms, bamboo shoots and *tofu,* and cook 3–4 minutes or until the vegetables are half-tender. (Tofu has a consistency much like thick custard. It should be handled carefully to avoid breaking. Canned bamboo shoots and *shirataki* are used without advance preparation.) Add meat and cook 3–4 minutes or until it loses its red color. Add the watercress but do not overcook. Serve with bowls of hot rice.

More of any of the ingredients may be added to the saucepan while the *sukiyaki* is cooking and being eaten.

NOTE: The juices in the saucepan are delicious spooned over bowls of hot rice.

TEMPURA

18   medium-sized shrimp
2   flounder fillets
1   medium-sized squid
6   sea scallops
1   carrot, scraped
12   long stringbeans

* The use of Japanese or Japanese-type soy sauce (*shoyu*) is recommended. Most other soy sauces, while excellent for other purposes, scarcely do justice to Japanese cooking.

** If *mirin* (Japanese cooking wine) is not available, use cooking sherry or port wine and increase sugar to taste.

1   sweet potato
4   cups vegetable oil or, preferably, 3 cups vegetable oil
    and 1 cup sesame oil
    Tempura batter (see below)
    Tempura sauce (see below)

Insert the small blade of a pair of scissors under the shell of each shrimp. Starting at the head portion, cut down to, but not through, the last tail segment. Peel shrimp, leaving tail segment intact. Cut off lower half of tail. Wash peeled shrimp under cold running water to remove sand and intestinal tract. Using a sharp knife, make shallow cuts across the underside of each shrimp in 3 equidistant places. This permits "straightening" the shrimp lengthwise.

Cut flounder into small sections measuring about 2 by 3 inches. Remove tentacles from squid and peel off outer and inner skins. Cut into square bite-sized pieces. Cut scallops into quarters.

Cut carrot into ⅛-inch-thick slices. Cut string beans into 3-inch lengths. Peel sweet potato; cut it into ⅛-inch-thick slices and cut each slice into quarters.

Dry all seafood and vegetables well between clean cloths or absorbent toweling.

Using a deep-fry thermometer or electric skillet, heat oil to 330° F. This temperature must be maintained for entire frying process. Hold shrimp by the tail, dip into batter (see below) and gently drop, one at a time, into hot fat. Deep-fry a few shrimp at a time until the batter is golden brown, or about 30 seconds to 1 minute. Dip flounder in batter and cook same length of time. Repeat with remaining seafood and vegetables.

Remove deep-fried foods to paper napkins or other absorbent toweling to drain briefly. To eat tempura, fried food should be dipped in tempura sauce.

Serves 6.

Tempura Batter

3   egg yolks
2   cups cold water
2¼ cups sifted flour (Mme Saito recommends
      Superior Veribest)

Combine egg yolks with water and mix well. Gradually stir in flour, stirring from bottom of bowl (preferably with thick chopsticks). Do not overstir; this is the secret of a light batter. Flour should remain floating on top of batter.

Yield: 3–4 cups.

Tempura Sauce

1   cup water
2   tablespoons bonito flakes (see note below)
⅓   cup soy sauce
⅓   cup *mirin* or ⅓ cup sake mixed with 1 teaspoon sugar
    Freshly grated Japanese white radish
    Freshly grated ginger (powdered ginger may be used)

In a saucepan bring water to a boil and add bonito flakes. Cook for 3 minutes and then strain. This stock is known as *dashi*. Combine *dashi* with soy sauce and *mirin*.

Pour a little of the sauce into individual serving bowls and let guests add radish and ginger to taste.

Yield: about 2 cups.

SHABU SHABU

4   cups water
1   2½-inch square *kombu* (sea kelp)
2   pounds well-marbled uncooked rib of beef,
        sliced paper-thin
½   Chinese cabbage cut into 2-inch lengths
1   large-size onion, sliced paper-thin
2   pieces of *tofu* (bean curd) cut into 4 pieces (8 pieces in all)
8   thin slices of carrots
8   slices of bamboo shoots
4   sliced raw mushrooms
1   bunch watercress
2   cups *udon* (Japanese noodles, preferably *kishimen*)

Bring the water to a boil in an electric skillet or casserole and add the sea kelp. Let simmer 3 minutes and remove the kelp. Continue to boil the water throughout the meal in order to cook the ingredients.

Arrange the thin slices of meat on one platter, the cabbage, onion, *tofu*, carrots, bamboo shoots, mushrooms, watercress and noodles on another. Let each guest serve himself by taking a piece of beef with a fondue fork, dipping into the boiling liquid and cooking it briefly, then dipping the beef into a choice of 2 sauces and eating while hot.

While eating the beef, add the various vegetables and cook briefly in the hot liquid, dipping into the sauce of one's choice and eating while hot. When all the vegetables and beef are eaten, the noodles may be added to the broth, heated thoroughly and served. Serve hot rice with *shabu shabu*.

Serves 4.

BENIHANA OF TOKYO

120 East 56th Street	*593-1627*
61 West 56th Street	*LT 1-0930*
15 West 44th Street	*682-7120*

These three Benihana of Tokyo restaurants are essentially steak houses with a Nipponese flavor. Housed in Japanese country inns, authentic down to the ancient traditional methods of construction, the restaurants do not have a conventional kitchen. Nearly everything is prepared in the center of the guests' table on the built-in hibachi.

Japanese folk music is played discreetly in the background. Hostesses in kimonos bow and smile. Service is polite and deferential.

Benihana serves lunch from noon to 2:30 P.M. and dinner from 5:30 P.M. to 11:30 P.M. There is no lunch served on Saturday and Sunday.

STEAK BENIHANA

For each serving use:
- 2 large mushrooms
- 1 tablespoon peanut or soybean oil
- 1 6- to 8-ounce sirloin steak, trimmed of all fat
  Salt
  Pepper
  Mustard sauce (see below)

Trim mushrooms and cut vertically into thin slices.

Heat griddle or electric skillet to 400° F. or place heavy cast-aluminum fry pan over medium heat 2–3 minutes. Brush heated cooking surface with oil. Add steak and sear briefly on both sides. Remove steak to cutting board and slice into narrow strips.

Reduce heat to 325° F. Brush cooking surface again with oil. Add steak slices and mushrooms and cook until meat is done to taste (1 to 2 minutes). Sprinkle meat and mushrooms with salt and pepper, then transfer to serving plate.

Serve mustard sauce separately in a small bowl to use as a dip.

Mustard Sauce

¼   cup dry mustard
¼   cup water
2   tablespoons heavy cream
¼   cup soy sauce
1   tablespoon sesame seeds
1   teaspoon grated lemon rind

In a small mixing bowl combine mustard and water to make a paste. Stir in cream and soy sauce.

Crush sesame seed in mortar with pestle and add to mixture with lemon rind.

Serves 4.

SHRIMP BENIHANA

For each 2 servings use:

8–10   large shrimp
       Salt to taste
       Monosodium glutamate to taste
2   teaspoons butter, room temperature
2   teaspoons heavy cream
2   tablespoons olive oil
2   tablespoons soybean oil
½   teaspoon dried parsley
1   lemon, cut in half
     Ginger sauce (see below)

Peel and devein shrimp. Sprinkle with salt and monosodium glutamate.

Blend room-temperature butter with cream and set aside.

Heat electric skillet or griddle to 325° F. or place heavy cast-aluminum fry pan over medium heat 2–3 minutes.

In a small bowl combine olive oil with soybean oil. Using a pastry brush, coat heated cooking surface with oil mixture. Add shrimp and sauté about 3 minutes on each side.

Brush with butter and cream mixture. Cut each shrimp into 2 or 3 bite-size pieces. Sprinkle with parsley and continue cooking 1 to 2 minutes. Squeeze a little juice from lemon over each piece of shrimp. Transfer to serving plates. Serve with ginger sauce.

Ginger Sauce

1	tablespoon chopped fresh ginger
1	large mild onion, peeled and chopped
½	cup soy sauce
¼	cup white wine vinegar
½	teaspoon monosodium glutamate

Place all ingredients in electric blender and blend at high speed for 2 minutes.

Or combine ginger with onion and chop fine. Then add remaining ingredients.

Pour into small bowls.

Serves 4.

Chapter XVIII

FILIPINO FOOD

≈≈

Restaurants and Recipes

UNTIL the immigration laws changed in the early 1960s, there were barely 4,000 Filipinos in New York. Since then, their number has more than tripled, and all indications are that it will continue to multiply.

Along with an increase in the number of Filipinos, there has been an increase in middle-class, well-educated Filipinos. Many more Filipino businessmen are here now. Many nurses and doctors have come on exchange programs. And Filipinos form one of the largest groups of foreign students in many of the city's colleges.

As more Filipinos arrive in New York, more Filipino restaurants open. And they bring the spicy, exotic cuisine that is the product of the many peoples who make up the Filipinos themselves—Malayan mixed with Spanish, Chinese, Japanese, Indonesian, Negrito and Moorish. It is a cuisine that deserves—and is getting—a good deal of attention from New Yorkers with adventurous palates.

Except for those who came to New York as sailors and settled in a colony near the old Brooklyn Navy Yard, Filipinos do not tend to live together in any one area of town. In the same way,

Filipino restaurants are not found bunched within the same few blocks.

THE PHILIPPINE GARDEN

455 Second Avenue   *MU 4-9625*

"Filipino cuisine would flatter even the most jaded palate," says Josefina Olavario, who, with her husband Olie, runs this friendly restaurant. The scenery is jungle flora and bamboo, and the menu is a collection of exotic but inexpensive foods selected from the various regions of the Philippines.

The Philippine Garden is open from 11:00 A.M. to 11:00 P.M. and on Saturday from 3:00 P.M. to midnight. Closed Sunday.

SATANGHON

½	pound package *satanghon* (noodles)
½	cup Chinese dried black mushrooms
1	tablespoon vegetable oil
1	medium onion, peeled and chopped
1	small clove garlic, peeled and minced
¼	teaspoon pepper
⅛	teaspoon paprika
¼	pound boiled or roasted pork, cut into thin strips
6	large boiled shrimp, peeled, deveined and coarsely chopped
1	cup shredded boiled chicken
1	cup clear chicken broth or stock
	Patis (bottled fish sauce)
	Chopped scallions

Place the *satanghon* in a large nonmetal bowl. Cover with water and let stand 1 hour. Drain when ready to use.

Place mushrooms in a second nonmetal bowl. Cover with water and let stand for 30 minutes. Drain and pat dry with paper toweling when ready to use.

Heat the oil in a large skillet; add onion, garlic, pepper and paprika. Sauté until onion is limp. Add pork, shrimp, chicken and drained mushrooms. Stir for 1 minute. Add the broth or

stock and bring to boil, then slowly add the drained *satanghon*.
Lower heat and let simmer until *satanghon* is tender. Season
with *patis* to taste.

Serve very hot. Sprinkle each serving with chopped scallions.
Serves 4 to 5.

PANCIT

½	pound *pancit* (cellophane noodles)
½	cup Chinese dried black mushrooms
2	tablespoons oil or fat
1	small onion, peeled and chopped
1	small clove garlic, peeled and minced
½	teaspoon salt
¼	teaspoon pepper
6	to 8 boiled shrimp, peeled, deveined and chopped
½	cup shredded boiled chicken
½	cup shredded boiled or roasted pork
½	cup shredded boiled ham
1	cup clear chicken stock or broth
1	cup shredded cabbage
1	small zucchini, shredded
	Lemon juice
	Sliced hard-cooked egg

Place *pancit* in large nonmetal bowl, cover with water and
let soak ½ hour. Drain into colander and rinse with cold running water.

In second nonmetal bowl soak mushrooms in water to cover
for 15 to 30 minutes. Drain and pat dry.

Heat oil in a large, heavy skillet. Add onions, garlic, salt and
pepper. Sauté until onion is limp. Add shrimp, chicken, pork
and ham. Cook, stirring, 1 minute. Add stock and bring to boil.
Add *pancit*. Blend, then add cabbage and zucchini. Lower heat
and let simmer until vegetables are tender. Sprinkle each serving with a little lemon juice and garnish with hard-cooked egg
slices.

Serves 4 or 5.

CAFÉ MANILA

248 East 52nd Street   *PL 3-6987*

Café Manila is a cafeteria by day, a restaurant by night. By day it is airy and clean, and the tables are luxuriously far apart. At night yellow tablecloths and candles soften the scene. Both ways, the Filipino food is exotic and inexpensive.

Café Manila is open for lunch from 11:30 A.M. to 3:00 P.M. Dinner is served from 5:30 P.M. to 11:00 P.M. On Saturday and Sunday it is open from noon to 11:00 P.M.

CHICKEN EN ADOBO

2½	pounds chicken, cut into 4- to 5-inch serving pieces
	Black pepper
2	tablespoons soy sauce
4	tablespoons white wine vinegar
1	clove garlic, peeled
2	tablespoons vegetable oil
1	medium onion, peeled and minced
	Boiling water
2	tablespoons butter

Sprinkle chicken lightly with pepper. Place in nonmetal bowl; add soy sauce, vinegar and garlic. Let stand 15 to 20 minutes. Drain and pat dry with paper toweling. Reserve marinade.

Heat oil in large skillet. Add chicken and cook, turning the pieces often, until lightly browned. Add onions and continue to cook, stirring, until onion is limp. Pour off as much oil as possible. Then add marinade and sufficient boiling water to cover chicken. Cover and let simmer until the water evaporates. Remove garlic. Add butter and continue to cook for 1 to 2 minutes. Serve over rice.

Serves 4 to 6.

PART VII

~~~~~~

*Mexican and
Latin-American Food*

Chapter XIX

MEXICAN FOOD

〰〰〰〰〰〰〰〰〰〰〰〰〰〰〰〰〰〰〰〰〰〰〰〰〰〰

Restaurants and Recipes

THERE are barely 7,000 Mexicans in New York (there are, however, many Mexican-Americans from the Southwestern states not included in this figure) and there are more than a million people from other Central and South American and island countries. But none of these others have offered New Yorkers food fare that has had the impact of the Mexican *taco, tostado, tortilla* and *enchilada.*

Despite their few numbers, Mexicans continue to open some very good restaurants. The oldest Mexican restaurant in New York is 35 years old; the youngest opened only a short time ago. Almost all of them have the casual way, the sun colors, the easy charm of Mexico itself.

EL PARADOR CAFÉ

325 East 34th Street   *679-6812*

The food like the setting here represents the best that Mexico offers. The feeling of old Mexico is enhanced by dark wood furniture, handmade tiles and splashes of brilliant red against gleaming white.

A Broadway steak emporium called Tad's, where the chefs work

in the window to tantalize passersby.

Owner Carlos Jacott has tried to cultivate the taste of New Yorkers for Mexican food. Judging from the crowds and the fun everyone seems to be having, he has done just that.

El Parador is open for dinner only, from 5:00 P.M. to 1:00 A.M. Closed Sunday.

GUACAMOLE

1	avocado, peeled and mashed
1	teaspoon lemon juice
1	clove garlic, mashed, or 2 teaspoons garlic juice
2	teaspoons minced onion
1/8	teaspoon Tabasco or 2 chili *serrano* peppers, finely chopped
1/4	teaspoon cumin seed
	Salt and pepper to taste

Combine ingredients and mash to a paste. Serve as a dip with *tortillas,* or serve as a salad on lettuce with salad dressing à la Parador.

NOTE: Cubed fresh tomatoes may be added to mixture if desired.

Yield: 2/3 cup.

SALAD DRESSING A LA PARADOR

2/3	cup condensed tomato soup
2	teaspoons salt
1	teaspoon paprika
1	teaspoon onion powder
1	teaspoon garlic powder
1/2	teaspoon pepper
1/2	teaspoon dry mustard
1/2	teaspoon confectioners' sugar
1	tablespoon Louisiana hot sauce or 1 teaspoon Tabasco
1/2	cup wine vinegar
1	cup olive oil

Combine ingredients, except vinegar and oil; mix thoroughly. Beat in vinegar and oil alternately, beginning with vinegar; mix thoroughly. Store in refrigerator.

Yield: 1 pint.

CHICKEN MOLE

2   3½- to 4-pound chickens, cut into quarters
½   cup olive oil
2   tablespoons paprika
2   bay leaves, crumbled
     Salt and freshly ground black pepper to taste
1   teaspoon oregano
     Mole sauce (see below)

Place chickens in a glass, stainless-steel or enamel pan and add the oil, paprika, bay leaves, salt, pepper and oregano. Turn the chicken in the mixture until parts are well coated. Cover and refrigerate 12 hours or longer. Occasionally turn the chicken in the mixture.

Place the chicken in the simmering mole sauce and cook 1 hour or longer or until chicken is fork-tender.

Serves 8.

Mole Sauce

½   cup peanut oil
2   cups finely chopped onions
½   cup chopped long medium-hot red peppers*
2   cloves garlic, peeled and chopped
½   cup finely chopped mushrooms
¾   cup finely chopped green pepper
3   ounces mole powder**
1½   tablespoons flour
2   cups cold water
1   teaspoon oregano
4   bay leaves
1   teaspoon monosodium glutamate
2   6-ounce cans tomato paste
5   cups fresh or canned beef broth
1   ounce Mexican chocolate**
     Salt to taste
1   tablespoon cornstarch (optional)

* A small amount of canned *jalapenos* or chilies *serranos* may be substituted. These fiery-hot chilies are available at Mexican food stores.

** Available at Mexican food stores.

Heat the oil in a large casserole or kettle. Add the onions, red pepper, garlic, mushrooms and green pepper. Cook, stirring frequently, until onions are golden brown.

Combine the mole powder with flour and stir it into the casserole. While stirring, add the water, oregano, bay leaves, monosodium glutamate, tomato paste and broth. Add the chocolate and stir until chocolate is dissolved. Continue cooking, stirring occasionally, about 2 hours. Season to taste with salt. If desired, the sauce may be thickened with cornstarch blended with a little water.

Yield: about 3 quarts.

NATILLA

1	cup sugar
3	tablespoons cornstarch
¼	teaspoon salt
1	quart milk
5	eggs, well beaten
2	tablespoons butter
1	teaspoon vanilla extract
	Cinnamon

Combine sugar, cornstarch and salt. Stir in ¼ cup of the milk to make a smooth paste. Add eggs and stir until smooth. Scald remaining 3¾ cups milk in top of double boiler. Add egg mixture slowly. Place over boiling water and stir constantly with wooden spoon until mixture thickens slightly and spoon becomes coated. Stir in butter and vanilla. Pour into individual serving dishes. Chill. Before serving, sprinkle on cinnamon.

Serves 6 to 8.

CACTUS SALAD

1	7¼-ounce can of cactus*
1	clove garlic, finely minced
1	tablespoon coarsely chopped red onion
	Juice of ½ lime or lemon
2	tablespoons peanut oil

* Available at Mexican food stores.

Salt and pepper, freshly ground, to taste
Tabasco sauce to taste

Rinse the cactus pieces under cold running water and drain well. Combine the cactus and all the ingredients. Serve chilled. Serves 4.

PANCHO VILLA'S MEXICAN RESTAURANT

1501 Second Avenue   *734-9144*

It's not very large, but what there is of it is very nice. The walls are white stucco and the beams are dark. There are tiled floors and antique light fixtures. Altogether, thoroughly delightful Mexican surroundings for good Mexican food.

Pancho Villa's is open every day from noon to 1:00 A.M.

ENCHILADAS SUIZAS

1	very ripe avocado, peeled and chopped
½	head Boston lettuce, chopped
1	8-ounce can green tomatoes (*tomatitos verdes*)
1	clove garlic, minced
¼	onion, minced
½	teaspoon salt
3	tablespoons butter
12	*tortillas*
2	cups diced cooked chicken
1	cup sour cream

Combine avocado, lettuce, green tomatoes, garlic, onion and salt in an electric blender. Blend at high speed until mixture is smooth. Melt butter in a shallow skillet, dip *tortillas* in warm butter to soften, lay flat on a plate and place 1 tablespoon cooked chicken in center of each. Roll up and place in shallow baking dish. Pour avocado sauce over *enchiladas* and place under broiler until very hot. Garnish with sour cream and serve hot.

Serves 4 to 6.

Tyro basketball stars get in a few passes at the basket for all to see

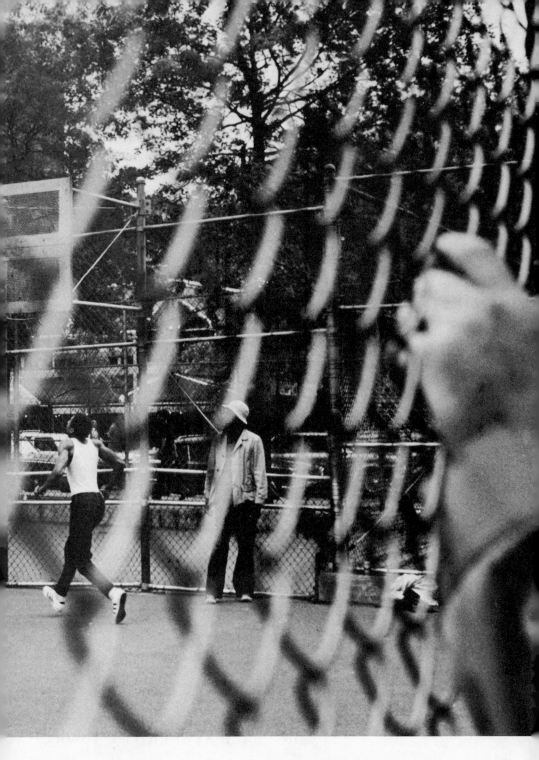

in the West Village.

CHICKEN TOSTADAS

  1   cup salad oil
 12   *tortillas* (room temperature)
1½   cups refried beans*
  2   cups cooked chicken, cut in slivers
  1   medium head lettuce, coarsely chopped
1½   cups red chili sauce
  2   avocados, peeled and sliced
     Juice of 1 lemon

Heat salad oil in deep, heavy sauté pan. Fry *tortillas*, one at a time, until crisp and lightly puffed, about 1 minute. Keep warm on a baking sheet in 250° F. oven until all 12 have been fried. Spread crisp *tortilla* with refried beans, cover with chicken slivers, and top with a tablespoon of chili sauce. Bake in a 400° F. oven for 5 to 10 minutes until heated through. While the *tostadas* are baking, peel, seed and slice avocados, sprinkle with lemon juice and arrange as a garnish on *tostadas* just before serving. Serve any remaining sauce separately.
Serves 6.

RED CHILI SAUCE

½   medium-size onion, finely chopped
½   tablespoon salad oil
1½   cups tomato puree
 1   cup water
 2   cloves garlic, finely minced
2½   tablespoons chili powder
¼   teaspoon dried cumin seed
½   teaspoon dried hot red chilies
 1   teaspoon salt

Sauté onion in salad oil until soft and golden. Add tomato puree, water and garlic and blend well; gradually stir in chili powder. Add dried chilies, cumin and salt. Cover and simmer over very low heat for 30 to 35 minutes, stirring frequently.
Makes about 2 cups.

* See footnote page 311.

CHEESE ENCHILADAS

3	tablespoons salad oil
2	tablespoons butter
16	*tortillas* (frozen, canned or homemade)
2	cups red chili sauce (see page 310)
1½	cups refried Mexican beans*
1	medium head iceberg lettuce, coarsely chopped
2	cups coarsely grated Jack cheese
2	medium onions, coarsely chopped
6	radishes, coarsely chopped

Heat butter and oil in a shallow, heavy skillet; fry *tortillas* 1 minute on both sides or until flecked with brown and slightly puffed. Heat the chili sauce in a second shallow skillet and dip *tortilla* in the hot sauce before placing on a large, flat baking dish. Spread half of each *tortilla* with a layer of refried beans, then a layer of chopped lettuce; top with a generous helping of grated cheese. Fold other half of tortilla to cover filling. Bake at 400° F. for about 20 minutes or until cheese has melted and *enchilada* is fiery hot. Sprinkle with chopped onion and radishes and pour remaining hot chili sauce over the top. Serve at once.
Serves 8.

* Boiled red kidney beans (or black beans) mashed and then fried in pork fat, seasoned with salt, pepper, and if desired minced onion. Canned beans may be used.

Chapter XX

LATIN-AMERICAN FOOD

~~~~~~

Restaurants and Recipes

"Aquí se habla español" is the most common sign in town. And rightly so. Today New York, with well over a million Latin Americans (and "Latin American" here includes all people from countries south of the border with the exception of Mexico), is one of the ten largest Spanish-speaking cities in the world.

The majority of the Latin Americans are Puerto Rican. And they are also the newest of the city's major ethnic groups. Although they began filtering into New York in the 1920s, it was in the 1950s, when air transportation between the island and the city improved, that large numbers began to pour in.

"El Barrio" in East Harlem is still the most important single Puerto Rican section of the city. But Puerto Ricans also live on the Upper West Side between 72nd Street and 145th Street, along downtown West Side and on the Lower East Side. Despite their numbers, though, there are still relatively few Puerto Rican restaurants and many of those which do exist are neighborhood luncheonettes.

The Cubans have established both themselves and their restaurants in many, though not all, of the same neighborhoods as the Puerto Ricans.

312

Other people, however, such as the Argentines and Brazilians, are operating well-established quality restaurants throughout the city and especially in midtown Manhattan.

There is one ground on which they all meet, and that is La Marqueta, the Park Avenue market that runs from 110th Street to 116th Street. There, among the plantains and mangoes, coconuts and banana leaves, yautia, annatto, akee and chilies, you'll find Puerto Ricans, Cubans, Jamaicans, Haitians, Argentines, Brazilians and all the people whose lives began in countries south of the United States.

ASIA DE CUBA

190 Eighth Avenue   *243-9322*

Mario Perez, manager of this neat and simple luncheonette, left Cuba for New York in 1961 with his Chinese wife. He also brought his Chinese chef father-in-law, who in turn brought his entire kitchen crew. Together, they set up one of the growing number of inexpensive Sino-Latin kitchens on the New York food scene.

The cooking styles are not mixed. You eat Cuban or you eat Chinese (Cantonese, in this case). But the clientele here is chiefly Spanish-speaking and Cuban food is more or less king.

Asia de Cuba is open from noon to 10:00 P.M. Closed Tuesday.

ARROZ CON POLLO

(Chicken with Rice)

½   pound salt pork cut into 1-inch cubes
¼   cup oil
1   3- to 4-pound broiler-fryer chicken, cut into serving pieces
1   large onion, peeled and chopped
2   tablespoons butter
1   clove garlic, peeled and crushed
2   cups uncooked rice
3   cups chicken broth or stock
1   teaspoon saffron

Brandy's, on East 84th Street on the Upper East Side, is one of many such pubby places where young New Yorkers gather to meet and eat.

1 cup dry white wine
1 8-ounce can tomatoes
  Salt to taste
1 package frozen green peas
1 small jar pimento strips

Place pork cubes in a large, heavy skillet over medium heat and cook, stirring, until fat has been rendered and cubes are crisp. Remove from oil with a slotted spoon and drain on paper toweling. Set aside.

Add oil to rendered bacon fat. Add chicken and cook, turning with a wooden spoon, until each piece is lightly browned.

In a separate pan sauté onion in butter until limp. Add to chicken along with garlic and rice; stir and blend. Then add chicken stock or broth.

Stir saffron into wine and add to mixture. Add tomatoes and season lightly with salt. Cover pan and cook over medium heat until chicken is tender and rice has absorbed the stock. Add more liquid if necessary to finish cooking. Add frozen peas the last 10 minutes of cooking time.

Serve garnished with pimento strips and the crisp salt pork cubes.

Serves 6 to 8.

FRINI FLAMENCO RESTAURANT

271 Amsterdam Avenue   *TR 4-8950*

For its first ten years, this small Latin-American restaurant was called Trini's. Alberto bought it and changed both the name and the scenery. Artificial grape arbors now hang overhead; there are bullfight posters on dark walls, a terra-cotta tiled floor and red tablecloths and napkins. The one thing Alberto has not changed is the excellence of the cooking, which ranges across Central and South America and occasionally over to the Caribbean for its inspiration. A flamenco guitarist plays every evening.

Frini's is open from 11:30 A.M. to 2:30 A.M. Closed Monday.

A summer's day, St. Mark's Place scene that seems like a stage

setting come alive in the East Village.

FRINI'S ALDILLA ADOBADO
(Barbecued Flank Steak)

2 pounds flank steak
1 clove garlic, minced
1½ teaspoons salt
¼ teaspoon coarsely ground black pepper
Juice from 2 lemons
Juice from 1 orange
½ teaspoon chili powder

Score meat on both sides. Combine remaining ingredients in a shallow nonmetal pan and marinate meat in mixture for at least three hours in refrigerator. Drain. Bring to room temperature; pat dry. Broil meat under high flame for 5 minutes on each side, brushing occasionally with remaining marinade. Cut into thin diagonal slices and serve with broiled bananas sprinkled with cinnamon.

THE JAMAICAN RESTAURANT
432 Avenue of the Americas   *982-3260*

West Indian art and music plus an island setting is the background here for the spicy—but not hot—Jamaican cuisine. The food is as authentic as you can get this far removed from Jamaica and its fresh, exotic island fruits.

The Jamaican is open from 4:00 P.M. to midnight and on Saturday and Sunday until 2:00 A.M.

CALALU

1 4-pound chicken, quartered
2 medium onions, peeled and chopped
2 medium carrots, scraped and chopped
1 medium green pepper, seeded and sliced
2 ribs celery with leaves, chopped
1 bay leaf
1 clove garlic, peeled and minced
1 teaspoon salt

¼	teaspoon black pepper
1	1-pound can Jamaican *calalu*
12	small shrimp, peeled and deveined
1	tablespoon flour
1	tablespoon butter
1	8-ounce can crab meat, flaked and all shell removed

Place chicken in a large stew pot, add cold water to cover and bring to a full boil. Skim surface until clear, then lower heat and add onions, carrots, green pepper, celery, bay leaf and garlic. Season with salt and pepper. Let simmer until chicken meat is very tender. Take chicken from stock, remove meat from bone and cut into small pieces. Refrigerate, covered, until ready to use.

Strain stock into a large bowl and place in refrigerator until all fat rises to surface and congeals. Remove and discard fat. Place chicken meat and stock in soup kettle over medium heat and bring to boil, then lower heat to simmer. Add shrimp.

Mix flour and butter to a smooth ball. Add to stock and stir until liquid begins to thicken. Stir in *calalu* and cook a final 5 or 6 minutes. Stir in crab meat and cook only until hot. Serve in large soup bowls with a mound of rice in the center of each.

Serves 8 to 10.

CODFISH AND AKEE

1	pound salted codfish
3	strips bacon, chopped
1	tablespoon coconut oil
1	medium onion, peeled and sliced
1	medium green pepper, seeded and cut into strips
1	clove garlic, peeled and minced
	Pinch of thyme
¼	teaspoon black pepper
1	1-pound can akee, drained
	Paprika
1	large tomato, seeded and chopped (room temperature)

Place cod in a glass or other nonmetal bowl, cover with cold water and let soak 12 hours or longer. Drain and rinse under cold running water. Place in a large skillet and add enough water to cover plus 1 inch. Bring to a boil, then lower heat and let simmer for 15 to 20 minutes or until fish flakes easily when touched with a fork. Drain thoroughly.

In a large skillet fry bacon in coconut oil until glossy. Add onions and green pepper and cook, stirring often, until onion is transparent. Place codfish over vegetables and sprinkle with garlic, thyme and pepper. Place drained akee over fish. Cover and cook over low heat until akee is thoroughly heated. Sprinkle with paprika and top each serving with a little chopped tomato. Serve with boiled green bananas.

Serves 6.

PLANTER'S CAKE

1	8- or 9-inch sponge-cake layer (homemade or from a good bakery)
¾	cup dark Jamaican rum
¼	pound butter (room temperature)
2	egg yolks
2	cups confectioners' sugar (more if needed)
2	egg whites
	Walnut halves

Cut sponge-cake layer through the center into 2 thin layers. Sprinkle each layer with ¼ cup of rum and set aside.

Place butter in a large mixing bowl and beat with electric mixer at low speed until light and fluffy. Add egg yolks and continue to beat until well blended with butter. Add confectioners' sugar alternately with remaining rum, beating well after each addition. Continue to beat until smooth, adding more sugar if needed to make a smooth but thick mixture. In separate bowl beat egg whites until stiff, then gently fold into first mixture. Spread between and on top and sides of cake layers. Garnish cake with walnut halves. Let stand 2 to 3 hours before serving.

Serves 6 to 8.

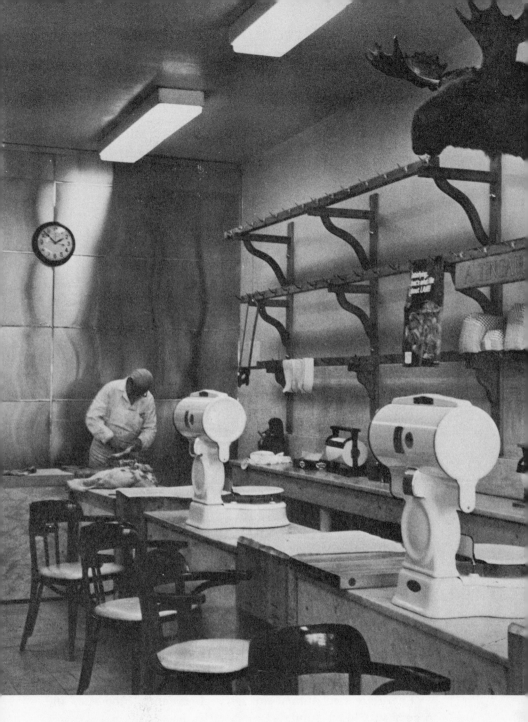

A. Tingaud & Sons, one of the oldest butcher shops in New York, is on Second Avenue near 57th Street. The meat is never on view but is brought out from the refrigerators on request.

LA CABANA

146 East 57th Street 758-3242

Potted palms and globe lamps in this Argentine restaurant give it the atmosphere of a cool, dim oasis. The food is authentically Argentine and the service authentically Latin.

La Cabana serves lunch from noon to 3:00 P.M. and dinner from 5:30 P.M. to midnight. Closed Sunday.

LA CABANA

(Argentine Custard)

¼ cup sugar
1 cup boiling water
3 eggs, well beaten
1 can sweetened condensed milk

Melt sugar in heavy skillet until it turns into a thin brown syrup. Gradually add boiling water, stirring constantly. Continue to stir until sugar is dissolved. Allow to cool slightly. Combine eggs and condensed milk and mix well. Stir in syrup and blend rapidly. Pour into one-quart mold, cover tightly with foil, and place on rack in large heavy kettle. Add boiling water to ½ inch below mold. Cover kettle and let steam for 45 minutes, barely simmering. Cool before turning out of mold. Serves 6.

CASA BRASIL RESTAURANT

406 East 85th Street BU 8-5284

It's like being invited to dinner in a private home with about 20 other guests. The tablecloths are bright cotton prints, the flowers are fresh and there is no menu. The food comes to your table as an agreeable surprise. On Wednesday, though, you can be sure of getting *feijoada,* the national dish of Brazil.

There are two dinner sittings each evening: 7:00 P.M. and 9:30 P.M. Closed Sunday.

FEIJOADA

3 cups dried black beans
¾ pound dried beef (jerked beef)
1 pig's foot
1 pound smoked pork
1 1- to 1½-pound beef tongue, smoked
¼ pound salt pork, blanched* and diced
1 pound smoked sausage
2 shallots, chopped
1 large onion, peeled and chopped
1 clove garlic, minced
¼ teaspoon cayenne pepper
Cooked rice
2 large oranges, peeled and cut into sections
Parsley

Wash beans well and soak overnight in enough water completely to cover. Place dried beef in nonmetal bowl. Cover with water and also soak overnight.

Place the beans and the water in which they were soaked in a deep, heavy enamelized cast-iron kettle and place over low heat, adding more water as needed. Cut the dried beef into 2-inch cubes and add to beans. Scrub the pig's foot well and add to mixture. Add smoked pork. Clean and add whole tongue. Cook, just barely simmering, for 2 to 3 hours or until beans and meat are tender. Remove tongue from kettle, peel and cut into 2-inch cubes; return to mixture.

Fry the salt pork in a heavy skillet, drain on paper towels and reserve. Cut the sausage into 1-inch cubes and sauté in the rendered fat until lightly browned. Add shallots, onions and garlic, and cook over low heat until transparent. Add 1 cup of the cooked beans and blend well, mashing the beans to a smooth paste. Add cayenne pepper and 1 cup of the bean liquor. Blend and simmer for 5 to 10 minutes. Drain beans and meat and arrange on a large platter. Pour sauce over all and surround with a border of hot cooked white rice. Garnish with fresh orange sections, parsley and the salt pork cubes.

Serves 10–12.

* To blanch salt pork, boil for 5 to 10 minutes in water deep enough to cover. Drain and pat dry with paper toweling.

BRASILIAN NUT CAKE

2	cups shelled pecans
3	tablespoons bread crumbs
6	egg whites
1	cup sugar
4	egg yolks
¾	cup sugar
1	teaspoon vanilla extract
1	cup cream, whipped
1	teaspoon orange liqueur

Preheat oven to 350° F.

Grind the pecan-nut meats in a blender. Combine with bread crumbs. Beat egg whites until almost stiff but not dry; add the 1 cup sugar and continue to beat just until stiff and glossy.

In a separate bowl combine egg yolks and the ¾ cup sugar and beat until thick and lemon-colored. Blend in vanilla. Fold beaten whites into yolks; fold in ground nuts and bread crumbs. Carefully fold to blend. Pour into well-buttered cake tins and bake 25 to 30 minutes. Cool on wire rack; when completely cool, frost with whipped cream flavored with the orange liqueur. Refrigerate until ready to serve.

Serves 6–8.

BRAZILIAN COFFEE RESTAURANT

45 West 46th Street   *PL 7-9352*

A bit of Rio de Janeiro in New York, the Brazilian Coffee Restaurant offers good native food in a conventional setting.

The restaurant was originally a mecca for Brazilian and Portuguese people (Brazilian cooking is largely derived from Portuguese cuisine) hungry for a savory taste of home. Because there is an emphasis on that American standby, meat, the restaurant quickly attracted a large local following.

Brazilian Coffee Restaurant is open from noon to 10:00 P.M. Closed Sunday.

A Sunday fisherlady trying her luck in the Hudson River not far upriver from the 79th Street boat basin.

BAKED BANANAS

8 bananas
   Juice from 2 oranges
   Juice from 1 lemon
¼ cup brown sugar
⅛ teaspoon salt
2 tablespoons butter
½ teaspoon cinnamon
¾ cup freshly grated coconut

Peel bananas and cut in half lengthwise. Place in shallow non-metal baking dish. Blend fruit juices with sugar and salt and pour over bananas. Dot with butter and sprinkle with cinnamon. Bake in preheated 400° F. oven for 15 to 20 minutes. Sprinkle with fresh coconut and serve warm.

Serves 4.

LA TAZA DE ORO

96 Eighth Avenue   *243-9946*

If decor meant everything, this plain and simple neighborhood luncheonette would be nothing, but owner Alex Vargas sees to it that the interesting Puerto Rican cuisine is well done indeed and the service is fast and friendly.

La Taza de Oro is open from 7:00 A.M. to midnight. On Sunday it closes at 10:00 P.M.

PLÁTANOS

6 plantains*
1 pint cooking oil
   Salt

Peel plantains and cut diagonally into ½-inch slices.

Heat oil in a large, heavy saucepan to 375° F. on deep-frying thermometer or until a small cube of bread will brown in about

---

* Plantains are large, firm green bananas grown in Central America and the Caribbean. They can be obtained at all Latin-American markets.

30 seconds. Fry plantain slices a few at a time for about 2 minutes. Remove with a slotted spoon to paper toweling. Pound each slice thin with the back of a wooden spoon or a meat mallet (like scallopini). Return slices to fat, again a few at a time, for a second 2 minutes. Drain on paper toweling, sprinkle lightly with salt and serve at once.

Serves 6.

ASOPAO DE POLLO
(Soupy Rice with Chicken)

2	cups long-grain rice
2	tablespoons lard mixed with 1 teaspoon *sofrito* powder
1	2-pound chicken, cut into small serving pieces
1	clove garlic, peeled and minced
1	small onion, peeled and chopped
1	half small green pepper, seeded and chopped
¼	pound ham, cut into 2-inch cubes
¼	pound pork, cut into 2-inch cubes
1	8-ounce can tomato sauce
5	cups water
½	teaspoon salt
1	package frozen peas
1	8-ounce jar pimento-stuffed olives
1	tablespoon capers
	Salt and pepper to taste

Soak rice in water to cover for ½ hour.

Heat lard in a large, heavy soup kettle. Add chicken pieces and cook, turning with a wooden spoon, until golden in color. Remove chicken and set aside.

Add garlic, onion, green pepper, ham and pork to kettle. Cook, stirring, over medium heat until vegetables are limp. Drain rice, blot dry with paper toweling, and add to kettle. Cook, stirring, for 2 to 3 minutes.

Pour in tomato sauce and return chicken to kettle. Add water and stir once to blend. Partly cover kettle and let mixture simmer very gently until chicken is cooked and rice very

Santa Claus ringing his bell on a wintry day along busy Fifth Avenue.

Saks Fifth Avenue and St. Patrick's Cathedral are in the background.

tender. Add frozen peas, cover and cook for a final 5 to 6 minutes. Stir in olives and capers. Correct seasoning with salt and pepper as needed. Serve in shallow soup bowls with plenty of crusty bread to mop up the sauce.

Serves 6.

PART VIII

American Food

Chapter XXI

AMERICAN FOOD

~~~~~~

Restaurants and Recipes

It's chili and beans in Texas, barbecued ribs in Atlanta, shrimp creole in New Orleans, steaks and chops in Chicago and Kansas City, lobster in Maine, beans in Boston and ham in Virginia. Who's to say what is American food?

Essentially, though, American-style cooking is derived from the English settlers, who adapted their food customs to what was on hand. "American as apple pie" it may be, but the pie originated in England and the idea of enclosing a filling between two pastry crusts goes back to the Norman invasion. The American versions of "baked" and "boiled" are first cousins to English fare, too. The "baked" may be blueberry and turkey instead of kidney and beef, but they are based on the same basic principles. As in any country, American food is a reflection of its climate and its people. When you have a country as huge and varied as these United States, no one cuisine can be truthfully considered to be typical. It's a complex subject. As soon as you say American food is not so heavily spiced as Spanish or Indian or not so intricate as French, you are reminded of Louisiana creole cooking or Southern barbecues. Nonetheless, the fact remains that few Americans will complain about a meal of roast beef or steak and baked potato with pumpkin pie for dessert.

Still resplendent as in the old days, Gage and Tollner's, near Court

Street, Brooklyn, serves good American food.

Miles of coastline stretching from the Florida Keys to Maine, from the Mexican border to Puget Sound, make seafood an inherent part of American cuisine, and a transportation network second to none puts Maine lobster on Missouri tables and makes Florida shrimp Nebraska's first course for a festive dinner. This same armada of planes and trucks rushes perishable vegetables and fruits from in-season California to snowbound Vermont. It's always the season, somewhere in the U.S., for something fresh. Florida and California ship truck-garden fare all winter long, and when it's too hot "way down South" for delicate vegetables, New Jersey and Connecticut farms are at their peak.

We tend to dismiss American food as being uninteresting, with too much reliance on "frozen" and "canned," and it's partially true, but in every country there are good and bad cooks, superb and not so good restaurants. The best of American cooking is often the best in the world, and few countries offer the variety that is indigenous to the U.S.A.

SWEET'S RESTAURANT

2 Fulton Street   *WH 4-9628*

The food is fish, simply prepared and simply divine, as it has been since Sweet's first opened in 1845.

Sweet's is still located on the second floor of its original building, amid old maps and seafaring souvenirs. About the only major change in decor in its 126 years are the electric lights, and even that happened back in 1882 when Sweet's was among the first 59 establishments in New York to be lighted by electricity.

Each day before dawn Sweet's manager is one of the first at the Fulton Fish Market across the street to choose the best of the day's offering. Nothing at Sweet's is frozen or canned. If Fulton Fish Market doesn't have it fresh that morning, Sweet's won't have it that day. That's the kind of rule that gives a place a fine 126-year-old reputation.

Sweet's is open from 11:00 A.M. to 8:00 P.M. Monday through Friday. Closed weekends.

SAUTÉED SHAD ROE

8   tablespoons butter
2   shad roe
    Flour
    Salt
    Pepper
    Lemon juice
½   cup minced parsley

Melt the 6 tablespoons of butter in a heavy skillet over moderate heat. Dip each roe in flour, then dust off excess and place gently in hot butter. Sauté one minute, turning them to coat all sides with butter. Cover skillet and cook roe for 10 minutes. Turn and cook second side 10 minutes. Sprinkle with salt and pepper. Remove them to hot serving plates. Add lemon juice, remaining butter and parsley to skillet. Increase heat and stir for a minute. Spoon over roe and serve at once.

Serves 4.

NEW ENGLAND FISH CHOWDER

1   pound halibut or haddock
     Bones from any white fish (such as halibut, cod, haddock)
1   onion, cut fine
½   cup chopped celery
½   pound butter
¼   teaspoon salt
¼   teaspoon curry powder
     Few grains of pepper
1¼   tablespoons flour
½   pint milk
½   pint cream
2   cups raw potatoes cut into fine dice

Wash fish and fish bones and cover with salted water. Bring slowly to a boil and simmer (covered) for 15 minutes. Drain, reserving stock. Remove skin and bones from fish. Set fish aside to use later.

These two unusually attired readers of New York's more unusual news-
papers go unnoticed by the customers at Ratner's who are eating the

dairy food people come for from far and wide.

Sauté onions and celery in ¼ pound butter. Add salt, curry powder and pepper. Then melt ¼ pound butter in a large saucepan and blend flour into it, stirring to make a smooth paste. Heat and combine milk and cream and slowly blend into this mixture. Add 1 quart fish stock, fish, celery, onions and potatoes. Bring to a boil and simmer until potatoes are tender.

Serves 6 to 8.

CREAMED SEAFOOD

3	tablespoons butter
2	tablespoons flour
1½	cups milk
½	cup dry sherry
2	egg yolks, lightly beaten
½	pound boiled shrimp, cooked, shelled, deveined and chopped
1	cup flaked cooked crab meat
1	cup diced boiled lobster meat
¼	chopped pimento
¼	cup slivered black olives
¼	cup Parmesan cheese
¼	cup buttered bread crumbs
	Toast points

Melt the butter in a large saucepan over low heat. Remove pan from heat and stir in flour. Then slowly blend in ½ cup of the milk. When smooth, return pan to heat and add remaining milk and sherry. Cook, stirring, until sauce thickens. Remove from heat and add egg yolks, stirring rapidly with a wire whisk as they are added. Add shrimp, crab, lobster, pimento and olives. Blend, then spoon mixture into 6 individual ovenproof ramekins. Sprinkle each with Parmesan cheese and bread crumbs. Place under broiler heat until glazed and bubbly hot. Garnish with toast points and serve at once.

Serves 6.

SCALLOP STEW

3	cups milk
1	cup heavy cream

½	cup dry white wine
2	tablespoons butter
½	teaspoon Worcestershire sauce
1	teaspoon sugar
½	teaspoon salt
¼	teaspoon white pepper
1	pound bay scallops, minced
	Minced parsley
	Paprika

Combine milk, cream, wine and butter in deep saucepan. Season with Worcestershire sauce, sugar, salt and pepper. Place over medium heat until scalded—near boiling point—but do not allow to boil. Add minced scallops and continue to cook for 4 to 5 minutes. Stir often; do not allow to boil.

Serve steamy hot. Garnish each serving with paprika and minced parsley.

Serves 4 to 6.

COOKERY LAFAYETTE, INC.

21 University Place   *OR 4-4450*

The "Cookery," as it is called by its affectionados, is a handsome clean version of a coffeehouse. In the heart of the most affluent area of the Village, it caters to the upper middle class tenants of the close-by high-rise apartments and to the town house owners. Sunday brunch is a favorite: bagels and lox, marvelous egg dishes and great Danish. Lunch and dinner specialties are available and their hamburgers are famous. Frozen cream cheese is a not-to-be missed dessert.

Cookery Lafayette is open from 11:00 A.M. to 1:00 A.M. seven days a week.

COOKERY FROZEN CHEESE DESSERT

2	cups cottage cheese
3	cups sour cream
2	cups confectioners' sugar
1	teaspoon vanilla

Two hungry New Yorkers bring their lunch to picnic at the South

Street seaport on the East River.

Mix all ingredients in an electric mixer or blender. Do not attempt to make this dish without this equipment; the product will not be smooth enough if blended by hand.

For immediate use, refrigerate in coupe or sherbet glasses until well chilled. Freeze for future use and bring to spooning softness before serving.

Top with preserves of your choice, preferably on the tart side. Serves 8.

NOTES FROM THE COOKERY BAR

The Martinski
(The Ultimate Martini, an Original Cookery Creation)

100 proof imported vodka, e.g., Stolichnaya (Russian), Kord (Czech), Zubrowka or Wybrowka (Polish)
Ice cubes
Thinly sliced red onions

Pour the vodka, to your heart's content, over the ice in a mixing glass. Stir long enough to chill, but not—heaven forfend—so long as to dilute. Strain over the sliced onion rings. Sip through a short straw, for the mingled flavor of vodka and onions. As a guide to the quantity of vodka that can be considered an adequate drink, the Cookery serves 2½ ounces of vodka, a fact that need not be an inhibiting factor.

Frutas Con Vino
(A Kind of Mexican Sangria)

Frozen sliced strawberries or sugared fresh berries
Rosé wine
Ice cubes
Soda

Fill a 10-ounce glass with ice cubes. Pour over them 2 or 3 tablespoons of strawberries; in this case, the frozen is preferable to the fresh. Fill to the top with rosé wine, leaving only enough room at the top for a few squirts of soda. Stir.

Sangrita

(The Mexican National Mary)

Tequila (100 proof is suggested)
1   2½-ounce can tomato juice
    Juice of 4 oranges
    Juice of 1 lemon
    Juice of 2 limes
1   teaspoon chili powder, or to taste
1   teaspoon sugar
2   teaspoons dehydrated minced onions
    Tabasco to taste
    Salt to taste

Mix all the ingredients except the tequila. What you do next is in the alternative, depending on the degree of your devotion to authenticity:

(*a*) Authentic: Serve a juice glass of the juice mixture, and separately, a shot glass of the tequila, and some lime slices. The method of consumption is supposed to be: a gulp of the juice, a swallow of tequila, and a taste of the lime.

(*b*) Nonauthentic, but by far simpler: Pour about 6 ounces of the juice mixture and 2 ounces of tequila over ice, stir, and serve either strained or on the rocks. Garnish with lime slices.

This recipe should be enough for double drinks for 2; the one-drink drinker, particularly the lone one-drink drinker, would be better served to choose a drink less time-consuming in preparation.

SIGN OF THE DOVE

1110 3rd Avenue   *UN 1-8080*

One of the handsomest restaurants in town, "Sign of the Dove" is named for an eighteenth-century inn that stood approximately on the same spot. If you like a romantic atmosphere, this is for you. Brick walls, slate floors, masses of flowers and plants; and, of course, candlelight.

O'Henry's Steak House, with gaslight and sawdust atmosphere, in Green-wich Village. It was originally a meat market, and you can see the meat hooks on the right over the bar.

Food and service are excellent, and the menu offers varied sophisticated American fare, along with "spécialités de la maison." Expensive, but worth it.

Open seven days a week.

Cocktails and dinner only, except on Sundays, when brunch is served from 12:00 noon.

SCAMPI WITH TRUFFLED RICE

12	jumbo shrimp
3	tablespoons olive oil
¼	cup Cognac or other good brandy, warmed
1	tablespoon butter
2	shallots, peeled and finely minced
½	clove garlic
2	tablespoons finely minced chives
	Salt
	Pepper
½	cup dry white wine
	Juice from ½ small lemon
2	paper-thin slices of lemon
	Truffled rice (see below)

Shell shrimp, leaving tails attached, slit down the back, then open and press flat, butterfly fashion. Heat oil in large, heavy fry pan, only until very hot but not sizzling. Add shrimp and sear quickly on both sides. Pour off excess oil, add warm Cognac and ignite. Take pan from heat until flames subside. Add butter, shallots, garlic and chives. Sprinkle lightly with salt and pepper. Cook, stirring frequently, for about one minute. Add wine; when wine is heated, add juice of lemon slices. Let cook a final moment and serve on truffled rice.

Truffled Rice

3	cups water
¾	cup long-grain rice
1	tablespoon dry sherry
1	tablespoon finely chopped truffles
¼	teaspoon salt
	Pepper to taste

Bring water to full boil, add rice, lower heat, stir once and let simmer until almost tender. Drain, cover and let stand until dry and fluffy, about twenty minutes. Melt butter in skillet; add rice, sherry, and truffles. Season lightly with salt and pepper. Stir with a fork until hot and dry.

Serves 2.

THE COACH HOUSE

110 Waverly Place   777-0303

About a century ago the Coach House was really a coach house. Today it is one of the finer American restaurants in the city. The menu carries a healthy number of American favorites, but owner Leon Lianides is a recognized gourmet, and the menu is also sprinkled with a few French and Greek specialties.

The restaurant is handsome, with red banquettes, brick and wood-paneled walls, a series of old American paintings, old copper cooking utensils and early American chandeliers.

The Coach House serves lunch from noon to 2:30 P.M. and dinner from 5:30 P.M. to 10:30 P.M. Lunch is not served on Saturday or Sunday. On Sunday the restaurant is open from 4:30 P.M. to 10:00 P.M. Closed Monday.

PEPPER STEAK

1 20-ounce boneless prime sirloin steak
   Fresh crushed pepper
1 ounce Cognac
2 ounces red wine
¾ cup meat glaze, sauce espagñol, or brown gravy

Trim excess fat from steak and render in preheated heavy iron skillet. Remove fat pieces after rendering.

Rub both sides of steak well with crushed pepper. Sear in hot fat (1 minute on each side). Reduce heat and continue to cook (5 minutes on each side for rare steak, 7 minutes for medium). Remove steak to warm serving plate.

Pour off excess fat and deglaze pan with Cognac and wine. Add meat glaze and cook over high flame until sauce thickens. Pour over steak. Serve immediately.

Serves 2.

THE COACH HOUSE
BLACK BEAN SOUP MADEIRA

    1   pound black beans, about 2½ cups, soaked overnight
            in cold water
    3   quarts water
    ½   cup butter
    2   ribs celery, finely chopped
    2   large onions, finely chopped
    2   tablespoons flour
    ½   cup finely chopped fresh parsley
    1   pound smoked pork knuckles
    2   leeks, white part only, thinly sliced
    3   bay leaves
    2   teaspoons salt
         Black pepper to taste
    1   cup Madeira wine
    2   hard-boiled eggs, finely chopped
    2   lemons, thinly sliced

Drain the black beans and place them in a large kettle with the water. Bring to a boil. Cover and cook over low heat for 1½ hours. Melt the butter in a saucepan and sauté the celery and onions for 10 minutes or until soft and transparent. Stir in the flour and parsley, continuing to cook and stir for 1 minute longer. Add the mixture to the beans, along with the smoked pork knuckles, leeks, bay leaves, salt and pepper. Simmer for 3 hours. Remove and discard the pork knuckles and bay leaves. Rub the beans through a sieve, grind in a food grinder or puree in small batches in an electric blender. Return the beans to the kettle with the broth and add the dry Madeira wine. Heat the soup. Remove from the stove and stir in the hard-boiled eggs. Float a slice of lemon on each portion. Serve hot.

Serves 10.

Two musicians seriously discussing their art, going over a score in Washington Square Park.

PECAN CREAM ROLL

Cake

6	eggs, separated
¾	cup granulated sugar
1	teaspoon baking powder
1½	cups pecans, chopped fine

Beat egg yolks and granulated sugar together until thick and lemon-colored. Mix the baking powder and pecans together and fold into the egg yolk–sugar mixture. Beat the egg whites with an electric or rotary beater until they stand in stiff peaks when lifted with the beaters. Fold the egg whites into the batter, lifting the batter gently with a spatula from the bottom of the bowl until it is well blended.

Grease a jelly-roll pan (15½ by 10½ by 1 inch). Line with waxed paper. Grease the waxed paper and bake in a preheated oven (350° F.) for 20 to 30 minutes, or until the cake starts to pull away from the sides of the pan. Cover it with a damp towel and chill in the refrigerator. Turn the cake over onto the damp towel. Peel off the waxed paper that was on the underside.

Whipped Cream Filling

2	cups heavy cream
1	teaspoon vanilla extract
2	tablespoons granulated sugar

Whip the heavy cream until stiff. Fold in the vanilla and granulated sugar. Spread the whipped cream on the cake and roll (long side) like a jelly roll. Refrigerate. Slice. Serve chilled. Serves 12.

THE COLONY RESTAURANT

30 East 61st Street   *TE 8-6660*

Almost everything about The Colony seems to have been designed to remind you of its glory-filled past. Gene Cavallero bought The Colony in 1918 and made it society's darling. In 1960 his son, Gene, Jr., took command and continued the aura

The famous Old Fraunces Tavern, where Washington took leave
of his officers and which today still operates as it did then, as a

restaurant known for its good food and atmosphere.

of elegance. The famous barroom, where the Duke of Windsor once asked to have his lunch served and thereby began a custom, was decorated in blue and white stripes. The sedate dining room had its crystal chandeliers, and the tables on each side of the entrance were always reserved for the Astors and the Vanderbilts.

Unfortunately, The Colony closed on December 3, 1971, but there is hope that it will open again soon.

BEIGNETS SOUFFLES

1	cup water
¼	cup butter (½ stick)
1	pinch salt
1	teaspoon sugar
⅓	cup sifted flour
4	eggs

Bring water, butter, salt and sugar to boiling point in a saucepan over heat. Remove from heat, add flour, and stir. Return to heat, and when mixture boils again and rises somewhat in the pan, remove from heat and add eggs, one at a time, beating continuously. Drop bits of dough the size of a small walnut one at a time into moderately hot deep fat. Gradually increase the heat so that the little dough-walnuts expand as they cook. When they are a good, deep brown, remove to paper towels. Sprinkle with confectioners' sugar. Serve with sauce sabayon.

Sauce Sabayon

6	egg yolks
1	cup sugar
2	cups Marsala or sherry wine
1½	ounces rum

Beat egg yolks until light and foamy. Gradually add sugar and beat until mixture has a light, creamy consistency. Add ½ the wine, beat, then add the rest. Continue beating this in the top of a double boiler over gently simmering water until mixture doubles in volume. Remove from heat and add rum.

Makes 4 to 6 servings.

CHICKEN GISMONDA

- 2 whole chicken breasts, boned and split to yield 4 sections
- 1 egg, well beaten
- 3 tablespoons cold water
- 1 teaspoon salt
- ⅔ cup fine dry bread crumbs
- 1 package frozen chopped spinach
- ¼ cup butter
  Dash of nutmeg
- ⅓ pound mushrooms, sliced (tops only)
- 2 tablespoons sherry
  Vegetable oil for frying

Place chicken sections on cutting board and pound as thin as possible with wooden mallet. Dip them in egg which has been mixed with cold water. Then dip in bread crumbs mixed with salt. Let stand at room temperature for 10 minutes.

Cook spinach according to package directions and drain; add 2 tablespoons of the butter and a dash of nutmeg. Keep hot. Sauté mushroom slices in remaining butter for 5 minutes. Add sherry. Cover and keep hot.

Heat the oil in heavy sauté pan and cook chicken pieces 5 or 6 minutes on each side, turning them with a slotted spoon. Remove and drain on paper towels.

Arrange 4 servings of spinach on a platter, with a cooked chicken breast on each. Overlap mushroom slices neatly on each chicken breast and spoon some of the mushroom pan liquid over the portions. Serve at once.

Serves 4.

LA FAMILLE RESTAURANT

2017 Fifth Avenue   *LE 4-9909*

"You can call it soul food, yes, but we like to call it cooking American style," says Mrs. Craine of the dishes that she, her sister, Viola James, and her brother-in-law prepare and serve in their very popular dining room on the corner of Fifth Avenue and 125th Street.

Call it what you may—soul or American—this delicious home-style cooking has been attracting individual diners, whole families and private parties to La Famille for 13 years.

La Famille is open from 11:00 A.M. to midnight. On Sunday the hours are 2:00 P.M. to 10:00 P.M.

DEEP-DISH PEACH COBBLER

1	egg
1	cup sugar
1	1-pound can sliced peaches
¼	teaspoon cinnamon
¼	teaspoon nutmeg
¼	teaspoon allspice
	Butter
	Biscuit dough (see below)
	Vanilla ice cream

Beat egg lightly and add sugar, peaches and spice; pour mixture into well-buttered baking dish and dot liberally with butter. Cover with biscuit dough and bake in preheated 400° F. oven for 10 minutes; reduce heat to 300° and bake for an additional 25 to 30 minutes. Serve warm. Top each serving with vanilla ice cream.

Serves 6 or 8.

Biscuit Dough

2	cups flour
1	tablespoon baking powder
½	teaspoon salt
2	teaspoons sugar
¼	pound (1 stick) very cold butter, chopped
¾	cup cold milk

Mix together flour, baking powder, salt and sugar. Add butter and work in with pastry blender until mixture looks like fine cornmeal. Add milk all at once and bring together quickly with a fork to a stiff dough. Toss on floured board, then roll out with a floured rolling pin to ½-inch thickness. Cut with large biscuit cutter into rounds to completely cover cobbler.

Here is where you can get fresh horseradish grated to order: a pickle stand on Allen Street, New York's Lower East Side.

21 CLUB

21 West 52nd   *582-7200*

One of the world's truly great restaurants, "21" has an air of established luxury that is unmistakable. Solid and comfortable, "21" lives up to its reputation for superb service and equally superb cuisine. The menu is continental but heavily sprinkled with "21" specialties that are usually top-flight American fare. Very much a grand luxe restaurant, prices are high and reservations are a must. Open for luncheon and dinner Monday through Saturday, except during the summer months when it is closed on Saturday.

BABY PHEASANT ALEXIS

6	small baby pheasant
	Vegetable oil
2	carrots, scraped and diced
2	ribs celery, diced
1	onion, peeled and diced
1	bay leaf
	Dash of rosemary
3	tablespoons butter
2	tablespoons flour
2	cups chicken stock
2	shallots, peeled and chopped
2	tablespoons lemon juice
¼	cup white wine
2	tablespoons sour cream
	Salt
	Pepper
¾	cup seedless white grapes

Place pheasants in a long shallow roasting pan and brush each with oil. Bake in a preheated 350° F. oven for fifteen minutes, brushing occasionally with oil. Turn the birds every five minutes so that they brown evenly. Add to the baking pan the carrots, celery, onion and bay leaf. Sprinkle birds very lightly with rosemary. Cover and continue to bake until birds are tender, about 20 minutes. Baste occasionally with oil and cooking juices. Remove the birds from the roasting pan. Discard the cooking liquid and vegetables. Wipe out the pan; return the birds to it. Cover and keep warm. While the birds are roasting, prepare a sauce Velouté: Melt two tablespoons of the butter in a saucepan over low heat. Add the flour and stir until well blended. Slowly add the stock, stirring as it is added. Then continue to cook, stirring constantly until thick and smooth.

In a second saucepan, sauté the shallots in the remaining butter until they are transparent. Add lemon juice and white wine and let simmer for a minute. Remove from heat and stir in sour cream. Add this to the sauce Velouté.

Add the grapes and stir to blend. Then pour over pheasants in roasting pan. Return the pan to the oven until birds and sauce are heated thoroughly—about 10 minutes.

Serves 6.

OSCAR'S DELMONICO RESTAURANT

56 Beaver Street   *HA5-6071*

At its height in the late nineteenth century, Delmonico was considered one of the grandest dining rooms in the world, and stories of its famous guests and fabulous parties would fill volumes. The first Delmonico restaurant opened in 1830. The last one closed in 1923.

Years later Oscar Tucci reopened the old Delmonico restaurant in the financial district. It is a different restaurant now, of course, catering to the tastes of a different age, but the physical inheritance is there to remind one of past splendors. The entrance is flanked by two marble pillars the Delmonicos had brought over from the ruins of Pompeii. Inside, the walls are red-paneled and outlined by dark wood piers. Tall windows are covered by Austrian shades and the chandeliers gleam. Elegance, at least, is still in style.

Oscar's Delmonico serves lunch from 11:45 A.M. to 3:00 P.M. and dinner from 6:00 P.M. to 11:30 P.M. Closed Saturday and Sunday.

PAPILLOTE OF SOLE DELMONICO

    8   fillets of sole
    8   thin slices of fresh salmon
    3   tablespoons butter
    ¼   cup dry vermouth
        Mornay sauce (see below)

Cover each fillet of sole with a slice of salmon. Roll up and secure with cocktail pick.

Melt butter in a large skillet and add prepared sole in a single layer. Pour in vermouth. Cover and poach until fish is white and flesh flakes easily when touched with a fork. Remove from heat and gently transfer papillotes to 4 shallow oval ramekins. Cover each serving with Mornay sauce and place under broiler; heat until glazed and flecked with brown. Serve at once.

Serves 4.

Mornay Sauce

    ¼   cup butter
    ¼   cup flour
    2   cups light cream
    ¼   teaspoon salt
    ¼   teaspoon white pepper
    ½   cup freshly grated Gruyère cheese
    2   egg yolks, lightly beaten

Melt the butter over low heat, then stir in the flour. When well blended, gradually add the cream, stirring with a wire whisk. Cook, stirring constantly, until thick and smooth. Remove from heat and add cheese. Stir until cheese melts and blends with sauce. Stir a little of the sauce into the egg yolks, then pour this mixture into the sauce and quickly stir to blend.

Use for any vegetable or fish dish that is to be glazed under the broiler.

Makes about 2 cups.

The building on the right with the iron gates and the figures of jockeys adorning the balcony is the world-famous 21 Club, where real princes, industrial tycoons and great sports figures meet, along with the men who have made it on Madison Avenue.

SLOPPY LOUIE'S RESTAURANT

92 South Street   *BO9-9821*

Louie doesn't like the name of his fish restaurant. He isn't sloppy and neither is the restaurant even if it does get a bit out of order come the lunch crowd and the boys from the Fulton Fish Market across the street. Before Louis and his brother bought the restaurant in 1930, it was named The Fulton Restaurant but called Sloppy John's, after owner John Barbagelata. When Louie took over, he renamed it Louie's Restaurant. The fishermen, the fishmongers, the truckers and buyers insisted on calling it Sloppy Louie's. The more Louie protested, the more they insisted. So, as he says, "When I couldn't beat them, I joined them." And Sloppy Louie's it is. And a wonderful place to go for some of the freshest fish in town served with a healthy dash of local color.

Sloppy Louie's is open Monday through Friday from 11:00 A.M. to 8:00 P.M. Closed weekends.

HOT-HOT SAUCE FOR SEAFOOD COCKTAIL

2	cups tomato ketchup
¼	cup horseradish
1	teaspoon Worcestershire sauce
2	tablespoons lemon juice
2	to 3 dashes Tabasco sauce
¼	teaspoon freshly ground black pepper
	Salt to taste

Blend together all ingredients. Chill for one to three hours. If possible, use fresh, not bottled, horseradish.

Makes about 2⅓ cups.

STOUFFER'S

666 Fifth Avenue   *757-6662*

The New York branch of this remarkable chain (practically an American institution) is like most of its counterparts, a large, pleasant restaurant decorated in a vaguely Colonial

Americana style, with an overall atmosphere of homelike charm. The menu is true Americana, and if you are longing for such U.S. favorites as corned beef hash, fried chicken, broiled lamb chops or steak, you'll enjoy it; salads are crisp and good, the vegetables fresh—and be sure to try the freshly baked rolls and pies.

Stouffer's is open seven days a week from 7:30 A.M. to 9:00 P.M., Monday through Friday; 11:00 A.M. to 9:00 P.M. Saturday, and 10:00 A.M. to 8:00 P.M. Sunday.

No reservations.

APPLE WALNUT UPSIDE-DOWN PIE

⅓   cup brown sugar, very firmly packed
¼   cup butter
¼   cup walnuts, chopped
        Pie pastry for double-crust pie
3½   cups chopped apples (4–5 medium)
¾   cup granulated sugar
2   tablespoons flour
        Dash of nutmeg
⅛   teaspoon salt

Sprinkle brown sugar over bottom of buttered pie pan. Melt butter and pour over sugar; stir to combine well. Sprinkle walnuts over mixture.

Place lower crust on top of walnuts; do not break crust. Trim even with edge of pan. Now add the peeled, cored, chopped apples and fill shell. Mix the sugar, flour, cinnamon, nutmeg and salt, and sprinkle over apples.

Place top crust on pie. Trim even with pan. Roll top and bottom crusts under together. There should be no pastry attached to rim. Prick top in 5 places with a fork. Bake in a preheated oven at 400° F. for 45 minutes until golden brown.

Now for the "trick" for a successful pie. Remove from pan at once. Run knife around edge of pie to loosen. Hold plate over pie and quickly turn over, so pie will fall onto plate. Allow sugar mixture to drip onto pie from pan. Serve warm, with whipped cream on top.

Makes a 9-inch pie.

STOUFFER'S LEMON SOUFFLE

3	tablespoons butter
1	cup sugar
4	egg yolks
3	tablespoons flour
1/3	cup fresh lemon juice
1 1/2	teaspoons grated lemon rind
1/4	teaspoon salt
1	cup milk
4	egg whites
1/3	cup toasted slivered almonds

Cream butter. Add sugar gradually and cream together until light and fluffy. Add egg yolks and beat well. Add flour, lemon juice, rind and salt. Mix well. Add milk and stir. Beat egg whites until stiff and fold into mixture. Pour into oblong baking dish.

Set in pan of hot water and bake in slow oven (325° F.) for 40 minutes. Sprinkle with slivered almonds and continue baking at 350° F. for 10 minutes longer. This gives a slightly golden-brown color to top of soufflé. Remove from oven and cut into squares to serve.

Serves 8.

PICKLED GREEN BEANS

Make a day before use.

2	No. 2 cans green beans
2	small or 1 large onion
3/4	cup vinegar
1/4	cup salad oil
1	cup bean juice
2/3	cup brown sugar
1	teaspoon salt
	Dash of pepper

Drain canned beans and save the juice. Slice onions thin and separate into onion rings. Add to the green beans.

Combine vinegar, bean juice, salad oil, sugar, salt and pepper. Pour mixture over green beans and onion rings. Mix carefully so beans are well coated with liquid. Let stand overnight at room temperature before serving.

Chill the pickled green beans before using them in your favorite way. These keep well for several days.

Serves 10.

STOUFFER'S CORN CAKES

2	eggs
1½	cups cream-style canned corn (1 No. 2 can)
1	tablespoon sugar
1	cup crushed saltine crackers (10 double wafers)
2	tablespoons butter, melted

Beat eggs lightly. Add all other ingredients and stir until well combined. Use a ¼-cup measure, scantily filled, and drop mixture onto well-greased skillet (350° F. in electric fry pan). Fry the individual cakes 2–3 minutes on each side, or until golden brown color.

Serve the corn cakes hot from the skillet with plenty of warm maple syrup and a little butter.

Serves 6.

PARSLEY RICE SOUFFLÉ

2	eggs
2	cups milk
2	cups cooked rice
1	cup finely chopped parsley
½	cup melted butter
1	tablespoon finely chopped onion
½	teaspoon celery salt
1	teaspoon salt
¾	cup grated cheese

Beat eggs, add milk, and mix with cooked rice. Add melted butter, onions, parsley and seasoning. Place mixture in a buttered casserole dish. Sprinkle grated cheese on top. Set casserole in a pan of water and bake in a preheated 350° F. oven 50–60 minutes, or until knife inserted comes out clean.

Serves 6.

One of the many organic-food lunch counters sprinkled around town.

This one is in Greenwich Village.

THE FORUM OF THE TWELVE CAESARS

57 West 48th Street *PL 7-3450*

A Roman banquet hall replete with silver champagne coolers in the shape of Roman helmets, silver wagons, brass and copper service plates in bas-relief, starched napkins—and prices to match. The place is aglow with things flambéed and flamboyant.

The Forum is open from noon to 10:00 P.M. On Sunday it opens at 5:00 P.M.

COFFEE DIABOLUS

	Spiraled peel of 1 large orange, removed in 1 piece
	Whole cloves
1	cinnamon stick
2	heaping teaspoons sugar
1	*brûlôt* cup (6 tablespoons) dark Jamaican rum
3	ounces Cognac
2	cups hot double-strength or demitasse coffee

Stud orange peel with cloves at approximately 2-inch intervals. Place cinnamon stick and sugar over heat in *brûlot* bowl (or chafing dish) and melt sugar, but don't burn. Add rum and continue heating mixture. Fix one end of orange peel on a long-pronged fork and dip in the mixture for a few seconds, pressing the peel slightly against side of bowl with fork. Raise the orange peel so that one end nearly touches the liquid, and very slowly dribble Cognac down the orange peel. Ignite the end of the peel. The Cognac will burn along the entire peel and may continue to flame for 30 seconds or longer; cloves will burn a bright amber. When flame has died out, return orange peel to bowl. Add coffee and stir. Remove cinnamon. Ladle steaming coffee into *brûlot* or demitasse cups.

Serves 2.

Ethnic and Gourmet Food Markets

Most of the unusual ingredients listed in this book's recipes can be purchased from the following food markets. Those sources which are starred (*) will fill mail orders. All addresses are New York, N.Y.

CHEESES

Cheese Board   751-4963
835 Lexington Avenue
10021

*Cheese of All Nations, Inc.   732-0752
153 Chambers Street
10007

Cheese Unlimited, Inc.   AT 9-2022
1263 Lexington Avenue
10028

Cheese Village, Ltd.   989-0328
3 Greenwich Avenue
10014

COFFEE AND TEA

*McNulty's Tea and Coffee Company CH 2-5351
109 Christopher Street
10014

*Porto Rico Importing Company GR 7-5421
201 Bleecker Street
10012

Rohrs Coffee Roasting Establishment BU 8-5968
1604 Second Avenue
10028

FAR EASTERN FOODS

*Japanese Foodland, Inc. RI 9-3761
2620 Broadway
10025

*Japan Mart RI 9-9678
239 West 105th Street
10025

*Katagiri & Company, Inc. PL-5-3566
224 East 59th Street
10022

*Oyama's Oriental Food Shop AC 2-3100
1302 Amsterdam Avenue
10027

K. Tanaka Company, Inc. TR 4-6600
326 Amsterdam Avenue
10023

Wing Fat Company, Inc. WO 2-0433
35 Mott Street
10013

Wo Fat Company 962-7067
16 Bowery
10013

FRESH HERBS

Balducci Produce AL 5-2916
1 Greenwich Avenue
10014

Empire Fruit AT 9-2150
1188 Madison Avenue
10028

Charles Ferrari, Inc. BU 8-7507
977 Lexington Avenue
10021

Jefferson Market OR 5-2277
455 Avenue of the Americas
10011

GAME

Jefferson Market OR 5-2277
455 Avenue of the Americas
10011

Maryland Gourmet Mart, Inc. LY 5-1500
414 Amsterdam Avenue
10024

Ottomanelli's Meat Market OR 5-4217
281 Bleecker Street
10014

GERMAN, CZECHOSLOVAKIAN AND HUNGARIAN FOODS

*Bremen House, Inc. 288-5500
200 East 86th Street
10028

Hungarian Meat Center, Inc. RE 4-8787
1592 Second Avenue
10028

*Paprikas Weiss Importers
1546 Second Avenue
10028

BU 8-6903

*H. Roth & Son Paprika Company
1577 First Avenue
10028

RE 4-1110

*Schaller & Weber, Inc.
1654 Second Avenue
10028

TR 9-3047

GREEK AND NEAR AND MIDDLE EASTERN FOODS

*House of Yemen East
370 Third Avenue
10016

LE 2-3430

*Kalustyan Orient Expert Trading Corp.
123 Lexington Avenue
10016

MU 5-3416

Poseidon Confectionery Company
629 Ninth Avenue
10036

PL 7-6173

*Karnig Tashjian
380 Third Avenue
10016

MU 3-8458

There are also many Near and Middle Eastern food markets along Atlantic Avenue in Brooklyn, the principal Arabic-speaking area of the city's five boroughs.

IMPORTED FINE FOODS

*B. Altman's Delicacies Shop
Fifth Avenue and 34th Street
10016

689-7000

*Bloomingdale's Delicacies Shop
Lexington Avenue at 59th Street
10022

EL 5-5900

*Charles & Company, Inc.   682-8900
340 Madison Avenue
10017

*Hammacher Schlemmer   421-9000
145 East 57th Street
10022

*Macy's Groceries   LA 4-6000
Herald Square
10001

Vendome Gourmet Specialties, Inc.   PL 5-2224
420 Madison Avenue
10017

INDIAN AND PAKISTANI FOODS

*Java-India Condiment Company   CH 2-7246
440 Hudson Street
10014

*Kalustyan Orient Expert Trading Corp.   MU 5-3416
123 Lexington Avenue
10016

ITALIAN FOODS

Amitrano Brothers   LO 3-5924
534 Ninth Avenue
10018

Essex Street Retail Market   254-6655
106 Essex Street
10002

*Fretta Brothers (dry sausages only)   CA 6-0232
116 Mott Street
10013

*Manganaro Foods   LO 3-5331
488 Ninth Avenue
10018

*Trinacria Importing Company**LE 2-5567**
415 Third Avenue
10016

MEATS

Brevoort Meat Market, Inc.GR 7-2574
54 East 8th Street
10003

Nevada Market (European cuts)EN 2-0443
2012 Broadway
10023

A. Tingaud & SonsPL 2-4320
1070 Second Avenue
10022

SCANDINAVIAN FOODS

Nyborg & Nelson, Inc.EL 5-9141
937 Second Avenue
10022

*Old Denmark**PL 3-5856**
135 East 57th Street
10022

SEAFOOD

Fulton Market Retail StoreBO 9-9665
18 Fulton Street
10038

G. Imperato & SonsPL 3-2866
896 Third Avenue
10022

Mediterranean Fish Company279-7887
571 Ninth Avenue
10036

L. Petrosino Fish Market   227-5398
134 Greenwich Street
10006

SPANISH, MEXICAN AND
LATIN-AMERICAN FOODS

*Casa Moneo Spanish Imports   929-1644
210 West 14th Street
10011

*Maryland Gourmet Mart, Inc.   LY 5-1500
414 Amsterdam Avenue
10024

Park Avenue Mart (*"La Marqueta"*)
Park Avenue from 110th Street to 116th Street

SPICES

*Lefvar by the Barrel   RE 4-1110
(H. Roth & Son)
1577 First Avenue
10028

*Paprikas Weiss Importers   BU 8-6903
1546 Second Avenue
10028

Geo. K. Simis Grocery and Meat Market   BR 9-5514
529 Ninth Avenue
10018

*Trinacria Importing Company   LE 2-5567
415 Third Avenue
10016

INDEX